URBAN ALERT!

URBAN ALERT!
Emergency Survival for City Dwellers

By Mary Ellen Clayton
with Bruce Clayton, Ph.D.

A Paladin Press Book

Endsheet and interior disaster photos courtesy of
Federal Emergency Management Agency

URBAN ALERT!
Emergency Survival for City Dwellers
Copyright © 1982 by Mary Ellen Clayton

Published by Paladin Press, a division of Paladin
Enterprises, Inc., PO Box 1307, Boulder, Colorado
USA 80306

ISBN 0-87364-246-5

Library of Congress Cataloging in Publication Data

Clayton, Mary Ellen
URBAN ALERT!

    Includes index.
    1. Survival skills. 2. Survival and emergency equipment.
I. Title
GF 86.C54   363.3'49'091732   81-22472
ISBN 0-87364-246-5   AACR2

To the Hills and the Deckers
who need it.

Table of Contents

1. Urban Alert!

U RBAN ALERT! is for city dwellers considering making simple preparations to tide them
through short-term emergencies such as fires,
floods, blizzards, earthquakes, riots, tornadoes, chemical spills, blackouts, hurricanes, nuclear reactor accidents, or simply unemployment. Nuclear war, while not
exactly a short-term survival situation, is definitely one
possible emergency which people should be taking more
seriously during the uncertainty of the 1980s. So
pointers for living through a nuclear attack are
also included.

Most of these emergencies will last from one day to a
maximum of four to six weeks (like the aftermath of a
severe earthquake). Even in the worst local disasters, it
is usually only a few days before the emergency services
get on their feet. If you have prepared ahead of time, you
will be snug, safe, and weathering the circumstances
much better than most of your neighbors during this
time.

It doesn't take a lot of time or very much money to
make effective preparations. It does take some research
and experience, but I did the research and acquired the
experience so you won't have to. I wrote this book for
busy people who don't want to go to a lot of trouble, but
who do want to take some effective steps to protect their

families in case of disaster. When you have prepared according to the directions outlined in *Urban Alert!*, you will have taken those steps—and you'll be much more confident about your ability to deal with any emergency that comes your way.

What this really amounts to is personal civil defense. You may have thought that in a disaster the local civil defense people would step in and rescue you, but this is not always so. The civil defense establishment in this country is overworked, understaffed, and poorly trained. But aside from these obvious shortcomings, who is more capable of protecting your family—you or some government bureaucrat who has his own family to worry about? It is likely to take a while for the rescue services to get to you anyway, and you had better be able to rely on yourself. You will probably be much better off. Disaster relief shelters are attractive only to people who have no other choices. Personal disaster preparedness makes the difference between a person being a *survivor* or a *refugee*.

Why I Wrote Urban Alert!

My husband is Bruce Clayton, the author of *Life After Doomsday,* (Paladin Press, 1980), a very popular nuclear war survival manual. Although this excellent book has lots of in-depth information, its appeal is limited. In it Bruce recommends that people interested in surviving nuclear war move to a rural area and store at least a year's supply of food. This may be good advice, but most people can't or aren't willing to leave the city.

One day last spring, Bruce's publisher approached him with the idea of writing a book on short-term emergencies for the millions of city dwellers who worry about things like earthquakes and tornadoes, but who do not know how to prepare for them. Bruce was involved in researching long-term preparations and was too busy to write a book about short-term emergencies.

Over the next few weeks I thought more and more about the project and decided that it was something I could do. I have always been interested in teaching short-term emergency survival because I feel more people make preparations that are not too extensive and do not drastically drain the budget. We have many city-dwelling friends and relatives who are not willing to go to great lengths to prepare, but I am sure they would make at least some preparations if the subject was approached in a fairly easy and inexpensive manner. I wrote this book for them and the many others like them. I hope it helps.

What Is Personal Civil Defense?

Getting ready to meet a possible urban emergency is mostly a matter of preparing to do without utilities and emergency services for a few days.

It means having a small supply of food and medicine on hand because a blizzard or flood might confine you to your house for a few days. It means having equipment for lighting, heating, and cooking in case your power is cut off for any length of time. It means keeping a supply of drinking water on hand in case the municipal water system fails or becomes contaminated. It means having battery-powered radios and nonelectric forms of entertainment. It means investing in a portable chemical toilet for times when the sewer system is out. It means buying advanced first aid texts and supplies and acquiring at least some of the training needed to use them in case someone is sick or hurt and the phones don't work and the doctors aren't available. It means having fire extinguishers for times when you can't get through to the fire department, and it means knowing how to use a gun in case you can't summon the police.

In short, preparedness means being ready to step in and provide these services for yourself during times of disaster, times when society is too disrupted or too preoccupied to fulfill its normal roles.

It means being responsible for your own life.

2. Let Them Eat Cake

Marie Antoinette made her mark in history with her callous lack of concern for the starving French peasants. Our government today seems to have almost the same attitude she did. The bureaucrats have built huge underground strongholds in the countryside around Washington, D.C., for their own use in a national emergency, each stocked with a year's supply of freeze-dried foods purchased with taxpayers' money. What do they have for us under the same circumstances? If we're lucky, we might get a box of unsalted soda crackers baked twenty years ago. The spirit of the French aristocracy is alive and well, and living in Washington, D.C.

Laying in some extra food is the easiest and the most important part of preparing for disasters. If you are hungry, nothing else seems to matter much. On the other hand, if you have a nice little supply of food stocked away in your closet, you can be much more rational about whatever disaster is going on around you.

There is real versatility when it comes to storing food. You can have as little as a two-week supply or as much as a five-year supply. You can spend as little as twenty dollars for 100 pounds of wheat or as much as you care to. You can store canned, freeze-dried, or air-dried foods or a combination of all three. You can store your food for years, or recycle it every month. The choice is yours.

Each system has a trade-off in terms of cost, convenience, and taste. The type of food stored doesn't matter a lot if you are preparing for a six-week urban emergency. Just make sure to store some food.

There is one thing to remember when you are putting together your food stockpile. You are never going to lose on this investment. You can always eat it, and with inflation the way it is, chances for the cost of food going down are very slim. My family recycles a month's supply of canned goods every three months, and the price difference in only three months is astounding. On some items which we don't like as well, the recycling rate is about once per year, and comparing the prices of the old and the new cans sometimes reveals 30 or 40 percent increases. Stockpiling food really makes you aware of the cost of living.

Canned Food Stockpiles

My recommendations in this section are based on the assumption that you want to store enough food to handle your needs for two to six weeks. You should not be comfortable with less than a two-week supply of food under any circumstances, and if you want more than a six-week supply, canned food is not the best way to go.

In many ways, canned goods represent the easiest way to solve the food storage question since cans have many advantages. Firstly, canned foods are all pre-cooked, so you can just open them and eat the contents without additional cooking if you must. This may not be the preferred way of eating your meals, but in some situations, it could be very important to have this versatility. Secondly, canned foods are packed in water which will supplement your own stored water supply.

So don't throw away the liquid; drink it. You will also be recovering many nutrients which have dissolved into the liquids. Thirdly, storing canned foods is easy. Just go to your local discount grocery store and fill the shopping cart with cans. You might get some jokes about stocking up for the winter, but you can just smile wisely.

Once a salesgirl looked over a month's emergency supply of canned goods and asked me if I knew something she didn't. I said yes. It obviously made her a little nervous, but it needn't have. Stocking up is just plain smart.

I have not mentioned canning your own foods in Mason jars, which is very common in some parts of the country. It is an entertaining hobby and gives quite a feeling of satisfaction to know that you have canned your own foods, but it is not necessary if you are not interested. If you would like to can your own foods, many good books are available on how to go about it and what equipment to get. *Stocking Up* by the editors of *Organic Gardening and Farming* is one of the best. If you follow the directions to the letter, you will run no risk of food poisoning, either.

There are disadvantages to commercially canned goods, too. The main one is that you have to rotate or recycle the cans periodically. It becomes very important that you buy only the type of food you normally eat because you are committed to either eating what you have purchased for storage, or throwing your money away once a year. The canning industry is interested in preserving foods only until the next crop comes in, so there are few reliable statistics on how long canned goods remain edible. Shelf life is determined by several factors, one of which is what is being preserved; for example, tomatoes deteriorate faster than peaches do because their high acidity corrodes the metal cans.

We keep four times this one-week emergency supply of canned goods on hand at all times. We rotate all items at least once a year by using them in our normal cooking, then replacing them.

You need to understand that canned goods lose their nutrients gradually, so it is inaccurate to say they are good for 364 days and at 365 days they are no longer edible. We are careful to stamp the purchase date on our cans and put the newly purchased cans on the back of the storage shelf. This way we are always eating the contents of the oldest cans first. We can detect no difference in the food quality between our year-old cans and comparable new cans.

For those of you who don't have any idea how much a month's supply of canned foods might be, I am including below the list of canned foods my family keeps on hand. The items on this list make up a one-week supply of food for Bruce and me with some extra thrown in for our two-year-old son. We have found that this one-week supply fits neatly into a large cardboard box. Your supply should be expanded from this list to fit the size of your family and the expected length of an emergency. Make substitutions and additions according to the kinds of foods you normally eat. Remember, you are committed to eating these foods at least once a year to recycle them, even if you never need them in an emergency.

Emergency One-Week Supply of Canned Food

1 can tamales (15 oz.)
1 can chili mac (15 oz.)
1 can pork and beans (16 oz.)
1 can beef stew (24 oz.)
2 cans corned beef hash (15 oz.)
1 can raviolis (15 oz.)
1 can chunky sirloin burger soup (19 oz. ready to eat)
1 can chunky vegetable soup (19 oz. ready to eat)
1 can chunky split pea with ham soup (19 oz. ready to eat)

[LET THEM EAT CAKE]

2 cans luncheon meat
1 can chunk chicken (6¾ oz.)
1 can chunk turkey (6¾ oz.)
1 can chunk ham (6¾ oz.)
1 can tuna (6¾ oz.)
1 can beef chow mein (28 oz. with 14-oz. sauce can)

3 cans whole new potatoes (14½ oz.)
1 can whole kernel corn (16 oz.)
1 can peas and carrots (16 oz.)

2 cans fruit cocktail (16 oz.)
1 can crushed pineapple (16 oz.)
1 can apricots (16 oz.)
1 can peaches (16 oz.)
1 can grapefruit sections (16 oz.)
2 cans pears (16 oz.)
1 can pitted prunes (12 oz.)

1 can Boston brown bread (16 oz.)
2 tins saltine crackers (14 oz. each)
1 jar cheese spread (6 oz.)
1 jar jam/jelly/preserves (12 oz.)
1 jar creamy peanut butter (12 oz.)

1 package assorted cereals (eighteen 1-oz. boxes)
6 cans evaporated milk (for cereal)
1 can blackberries (for cereal)
1 can whole dehydrated eggs (Ready Reserve)

1 bag small candy bars
1 jar peanuts (8 oz.)
1 can (or box) shoestring potatoes
1 bag raisin boxes (ten 1½-oz. boxes)
2 boxes pudding cups (four 5-oz. cans each)

[11]

1 jar instant coffee (2 oz.)
1 box sugar cubes (16 oz.)
1 jar nondairy creamer (3 oz.)
4 six-packs canned soda pop (12 oz. cans—cheaper than
    canned water)
1 box instant orange drink packets (six 1-qt. packets)

Add miscellaneous items for babies:
1 week supply of formula
1 six-pack individual cereal packs

Also, don't forget anything else:
1 box dog food

    This list is just an example, not an ironclad rule for storing food. It isn't intended to be a balanced diet, either, just plenty to eat for a week. For the most part, we tried to stick with canned foods which would not require cooking or added water in order to be edible. We broke that rule to include a few items that just couldn't be had otherwise—like instant coffee and a can of dehydrated whole eggs for breakfast. The crackers replace bread in the diet and carry the peanut butter, jam, and cheese. The inclusion of canned soft drinks and fruit is primarily for water, though you still need to store additional water.
    One lesson we learned was to overstock the list and not fall into the trap of planning on having seven soda crackers per lunch. We routinely overstock in terms of both quantity and variety. On the last days of the week, we want to have choices about what to eat and not have to sit down to a dinner of apricots and evaporated milk.
    We also learned to continually alter the list to emphasize foods which experience had shown we could easily use and replace. We had cans of boiled onions on

Everyone in the family gets into the act when it comes to keeping the shelves stocked. Of course, treats are stashed away, too, insuring willing helpers. These shelves are organized with the oldest cans in the front and the newest in back.

the list for adding to stews, but found that we never used them in day-to-day cooking. Off they came!

You may think it odd that we included dog food on the list. We could feed the dog table scraps, if there were any, but for $1.50 a box why not include it? Also, there is an old survivalist stockpiling tip which says to stock up on dog food anyway, because when the disaster happens and you find that you've raided the kit for the candy bars, peanuts, jelly, raviolis, and soda pop, at least you will still have something to eat. It's better than starving to death.

We purchased four times this one-week supply in order to achieve our month's supply of canned goods. The entire month's supply cost about $140 in 1979. We didn't have a more recent figure because we have been constantly rotating the supply since that time, so to give you a better figure for your planning, we went out and bought everything on the list to see what the 1981 total would be. It came to $250 for a month's supply. Did you know that food prices have been going up?

Freeze-Dried and Air-Dried Foods

There are three main advantages to freeze-dried and air-dried foods. They are very lightweight, will store indefinitely, and will give you quite a variety of foods. Storing dried foods means that you don't have to worry about constant recycling and that the food will, on the whole, seem familiar to you.

But these foods also offer substantial disadvantages, and they may not be worthwhile for people who want only a short-term food supply. The main problem with freeze-dried foods is their high price. Mountain House has just come out with a one-week supply of food for a family of four at a cost of $195. Now, this supply does give you 2,200 calories and 65 grams of protein per day, a very generous supply of food value as emergency food goes, but it costs about twice as much as comparable canned goods.

The other problem with these foods is intrinsic to their long shelf lives: they have to be reconstituted with water. Therefore, you must store a lot more water for cooking dried foods than you'd need for canned goods. Freeze-dried meals cannot, for the most part, be eaten straight from the packages. Preparation is fairly simple, usually consisting of adding the food to boiling water, which means that you will also use more fuel in your stove preparing freeze-dried foods than you will heating canned foods. Heating takes less energy than boiling does.

You would be wise to do some experimenting in cooking with these foods before you need them. I suggest that you write to Survival, Inc. for their catalog at P.O. Box 5509, Carson, CA 90749, or call 213-631-6197. (I will refer to Survival, Inc. as a source of food and equipment several times in this book.) Get the catalog and then order a few of their sample packs to give you a wide variety of foods to taste.

There are two cookbooks you will find useful if dried foods comprise your food storehouse. *Culinary Capers: Cooking With Lo-Moisture Foods,* put out by Perma-Pak, is an excellent guide to using low moisture foods of any brand. *The Sam Andy Food Storage Guide and Cookbook* (United Commodities International, Colton, CA) advocates using its own brand of freeze-dried foods, but also has many worthwhile recipes for cooking all freeze- and air-dried foods.

You might wonder why some foods are freeze-dried and others are air-dried. Well, quite a bit of research and experimentation has been done on this subject by the

Air-dried foods (*top*) offer many products unavailable in freeze-dried form. The Ready Reserve line includes over 30 products ranging from apple slices to powdered peanut butter. Lasagna, diced pears, beef steaks, scrambled eggs, and ice cream are only a few of Mountain House's more than 75 types of freeze-dried survival foods (*bottom*).

various food storage companies and has shown that some foods are better preserved one way than the other. Most companies use a combination of both types of preservation to provide the best tasting and widest variety of foods they can.

The Basic Four

The *basic four* is a food storage system borrowed from the Mormons, consisting of wheat, dried milk, honey, and salt. It is the cheapest way to store extra food, other than gaining a lot of weight, and is amazingly inexpensive in these days of soaring food costs. The wheat can be bought for only $20 per 100 pounds, the salt costs only a few cents per pound, and although the honey and dried milk cost a few dollars per pound, the total cost is quite reasonable. The wheat and salt will store practically forever if they are kept dry, and the honey and milk will be good for several years at least. Low cost and long shelf life are the two greatest advantages of the basic four plan compared to the other emergency food stockpile plans.

Wheat is extremely versatile. It can be ground finely for flour to make bread, cracked to make cereal, sprouted for salad, and separated into starch and gluten to make meat substitutes, just to name a few of its uses. As for how much you will need, 100 pounds of wheat, 2 pounds of salt, 15 pounds of honey, and 25 pounds of dry milk will feed four people for a month. However, wheat is not a complete protein and is best supplemented with beans and other forms of protein to prevent deficiencies if it is going to be eaten for long periods of time. For four to six weeks, it may not be that critical.

The disadvantages of this food program are great, however, making it almost out of the question for

A clean trash can (*top*) will hold nearly 200 pounds of wheat. Inside the plastic liner, carbon dioxide from Dry Ice protects the wheat from insect infestation. Wheat is inexpensive and easily stored, but it takes strong arms and a lot of determination to grind it.

owners of small stockpiles unless they cannot spend very much money. Firstly, you need a sturdy hand-grinder and the muscles to use it. It takes a lot of work to grind wheat. Secondly, you need some familiarity with cooking with whole wheat. You can make fantastic foods just using the basic four, but the time to start experimenting is well before you are restricted to using them as your sole diet. If you are interested in pursuing this alternative of food storage, I highly recommend two books to you, *Passport to Survival* by Esther Dickey and *Wheat for Man, Why and How* by Vernice G. Rosenvall. You don't have to be starving to appreciate the recipes in these books.

The third disadvantage to the basic four is one which has come out of the closet due to the popularity of high-fiber breakfast cereals. The sudden introduction of a diet of high-fiber whole wheat may cause some uncomfortable changes in bathroom habits. Be forewarned. If you have a very sensitive digestive system, you might just store white flour instead of the wheat. Throw in a few vitamin tablets, too. After the wheat is ground, it loses many of its nutrients, hence the need for the additional vitamins. The flour will take up about 50 percent more storage space than unground wheat.

Of course, if you don't like wheat, you can always store beans and other bulk staples instead. I met a bean salesman once who told me that although dried beans cost about three times more than bulk wheat, the price per pound, once the beans are soaked, is about the same and the protein content of beans is higher.

One other point about the basic four should be mentioned. Because the cost of wheat is so cheap, it provides you with an opportunity to perform a community service. Since this book is about surviving a short-term urban or suburban crisis, consider this: For about three hundred dollars and the cost of a small storage tank for the backyard, you can buy enough wheat to feed fifty neighbors for a month. Think it over at least. Suggest it to various groups.

So there you have it. Your choices are canned foods, dried foods, or variations on the basic four. Choose whichever you will, but do store some food. Don't fool yourself into thinking that you already have enough food on hand unless you have counted the meals on your shelves. You might find that all you really have is salad dressing and popcorn. Also, don't count the food in your freezer unless you have a way to can or smoke it in a hurry. Once the electricity goes out, you have about two days before the meat starts spoiling. Do something now while it is still relatively easy to prepare.

3. And Not a Drop to Drink

Though you must store food ahead of time, the lack of water will be the need more quickly felt. Most people can live several weeks without food, but only about three days without water. It's natural to feel an urge to panic when you turn on the water tap and nothing comes out.

You already have quite a bit of water in the house, most of which you probably never think about. There is water in your canned foods, especially canned fruits, and if you are lucky, you may have some soft drinks on hand. There is also drinkable water in the tank of your toilet (not the bowl) and trapped in your hot water heater. While you are thinking about it, why not turn off your hot water heater, find the drain, open it, and catch the water in a container? Practice now while you have the opportunity to learn from your mistakes. Just be sure to close the drain and open the valve again when you are through, and don't forget the pilot light.

After a few days, this incidental supply of water will be exhausted and unreplenishable, however, and you will need to drink water from one of two sources: stored water or purified, available water. The easiest alternative is to purchase some type of water purifier to make use of a guaranteed supply of water nearby. A swimming pool, lake, or stream in the vicinity will probably suffice, though you should store at least a few gallons of water for use during the first few days while things settle down. Remember that earthquakes may crack swimming pools. If you are worried about nuclear fallout, you should store enough water so you don't have to go out during the dangerous fallout period which will last two weeks to a month.

In an emergency, you will not want to experiment with water which may make you sick. You will probably not have access to doctors or medications and should take precautions to purify questionable water before use.

Several kinds of water purifiers are available. One of the cheapest and smallest filters is the Super Straw Water Washer. It costs $9.95 (1981) and will remove most odor, color, taste, and chlorine in ten gallons of water. The main advantage of this filter is that it is very portable, since it consists of a straw the size of an eight-inch piece of broomstick and a little bottle of chlorine bleach. You can easily put it in your pocket and have it with you when you are away from home. Its main drawback is that it treats only ten gallons of water, which isn't much water.

Another device is Survival Inc.'s Arnold Water Purifier. It is a little more expensive at $37.50 (1981), and though it recommends using chlorine bleach to kill microorganisms, it does not provide any. The filter is impregnated with silver in the charcoal for additional germicidal action, and must be activated with three quarts of water and two tablespoons of vinegar before its first use. I consider this its major drawback. What if you are out of vinegar or bleach? The advantage of this particular device is that it will filter fifteen hundred gallons of water if you are using water which is not too contaminated to begin with. This would supply a family

The Arnold Water Washer is a compact unit about the size of a
Thermos bottle, but will purify as much as 1,500 gallons of
drinking water. The Super Straw (*front*) will purify only
about 10 gallons of water, but it is small enough to fit in your
pocket.

of four for a year if they were extremely frugal with their water. That is a substantial plus.

The best type of filter for purifying water which has been contaminated with nuclear fallout is one made of earth. Buy a copy of Cresson Kearny's *Nuclear War Survival Skills* (The American Security Council Education Foundation, Boston, VA 22713) and make the filter described. It's easy to make from materials you probably have at hand, and best of all, it filters out more radioactive chemicals than the commercial purifiers do. It just takes a little of your time and initiative to make it.

If you don't have an outside source of water nearby, and even if you do, you will want to store water in your home. There are several ways to go about it, each varying in cost, ease of use, amount of storage space required, and, of course, the amount of water stored.

The first question you need to answer is how much water you must store. A good rule of thumb is to store at least two gallons per person per day. This will give you enough water to drink, cook with, wash your hands and face with, and even wash dishes with occasionally if you are careful not to waste any. I used to recommend storing only one gallon per person per day, but I had to revise that after taking the Three-Day Test discussed in chapter 12. We were very frugal with our water, but the three of us used five gallons per day. Test it out before being too sure of your family's needs.

Conserving water can become a fine art, and involves such methods as rinsing the already scrubbed dishes in a pot of clean water and saving this very slightly soapy water. Reheated, some of it can be used for washing your face and hands before you add detergent to the rest for scrubbing the current crop of dishes. Finally, the dishwater can be strained and added to the bathing water for use in flushing the toilet. You'll be amazed how far a gallon of water will go when it is reused four times!

The estimate of two gallons of water per day for each person presupposes that your physical activity will be limited and the temperature will be moderate. If you are doing hard physical labor, or it is 100 degrees in the shade, you will need quite a bit more water and you should store enough so you do not have to ration your drinking supply. Not drinking enough fluid can cause serious health problems since your body needs water (and lots of it) to function.

Once you have decided how much water to store, the question is how to store it. There are several ways, but the major difficulty in storing water is that it is extremely heavy. One gallon weighs eight pounds, so when storing a large amount of water in containers inside your house, you must make sure the floor is very sturdy. Resting the water containers on a concrete slab such as the basement or garage floor is best.

Several authors suggest putting water in glass jars and sealing them. This will certainly work, but the jars are expensive, heavy, and difficult to stack. They also may break during earthquakes. If you have empty jars and want to use them, go ahead. Do not, however, store water in metal containers, because it picks up the taste of the container and becomes somewhat unpalatable. Avoid storing water in secondhand jars that were not originally intended for food. Storing your water in liquid drain opener bottles wouldn't be very smart.

I have found that the cheapest way to store water is in one-gallon plastic milk containers. They are free after you have finished the milk and, once they are washed out and rinsed with a little bleach and a lot of water, they are ideal. They are also quite sturdy, though you should check them occasionally for splits and leaks.

Meet the Clayton survival bed (*right*). We put a 200-gallon air-frame waterbed mattress on top of 16 cases of emergency foods to give us a two-month supply of water and a six-month supply of food. Only bulky grains, beans, macaroni, and similar foods can be stored under a waterbed due to the warmth of the mattress.

We store our five-gallon water containers in the garage (*left*). These portable containers will give us about a week of readily available water before we need to draw on our other reserves.

The residual bleach in the water will probably prevent any algal or bacterial growth, but again, you should check occasionally. We stored fifty gallons of water this way for three years and had no problems. The only disadvantage to this method of water storage is that the containers don't stack well, and take up quite a bit of floor space. Bleach bottles work just as well if you thoroughly rinse them first.

If the problem of storage room is one you need to overcome, there are several solutions. One is to purchase commercially available five-gallon water jugs. With these you can store greater quantities of water in less space than with milk containers, but they are also much heavier and more expensive. Their cost ranges from four to ten dollars each (1981) and they come in various shapes, some more convenient than others. We prefer the five-dollar plastic jerry cans that look like military gasoline cans. Though five dollars doesn't sound like much money, you are paying one dollar per gallon for water storage which costs a family of four seventy dollars just to store one week's supply of water. The cost adds up fast, even though the water is free. Remember that five gallons of water weighs forty-five pounds, and many people won't be able to lift and pour from these containers.

There is another form of water storage I highly recommend. Store the water in a waterbed. We have two waterbeds in our home and find them very comfortable. It is especially comforting to know we have easy access to four hundred gallons of drinking water. I realize that many people have no interest in sleeping on a waterbed, but how about a compromise? Buy an inexpensive one (they range from $50-$200) and put it underneath your conventional bed. The space that is usually wasted will hold two hundred gallons of water with very little trouble. Before you take my advice, make sure your floor is sturdy enough to hold the weight of a waterbed which weighs about a ton, and keep a length of hose on hand for ease in draining the water. Check occasionally for leaks or algal growth. A waterbed liner might be good insurance too, though we have had no trouble with ours.

Incidentally, although waterbed dealers will press you to use algicide in your water, it is not a good idea if you plan to drink the water. We had our waterbeds filled with chlorinated Los Angeles city water for a year with no sign of algae. They have now completed another year filled with untreated Sierra spring water, and still no algae. Don't let the sun shine in the window on your waterbed and you'll have little trouble with algae.

You might find that the water you have stored tastes funny. This problem can be alleviated by aerating the water before drinking it. Just pour the water back and forth from one glass to another to get some oxygen into it. If it still tastes funny, run it through one of the water purifiers mentioned earlier.

At this point you may be asking yourself how much all this preparation will be needed. Well, my parents told me stories of having their water cut off during floods, of all things. The water supply became contaminated and they were left to their own resources for three days until drinking water was trucked to a central location where they had to go for water for an additional four days. This may sound like something that happened in a rural area long ago, but it was in Kansas City, Missouri, not too many years past. How would you fare without water from your usual supply for a week or more?

4. The Call of the Wild

Most of us have no idea how much we take for granted our sanitary facilities. I recently read John Barron's *MIG Pilot* which is the biography of the Soviet pilot who defected and flew his jet to Japan a few years ago. I was astonished to read that the majority of the people in the Soviet Union are still using pit toilets. This is a great contrast to Americans who flush the toilet several times a day with no concern about the five gallons of sewage created with each flush.

This book was written to help you live through a stressful time with the least possible disruption of your life. Squatting over a trench in the backyard is a major disruption! Making preparations for your sanitary needs is important. It isn't only a question of comfort— disease and death follow in the wake of poor sanitation. An extremely easy answer to the sanitation problem is a portable toilet available from Sears or Penney's. I can't tell you how strongly I feel about portable toilets. Food and water have to come first, but when it comes to essential conveniences, the portable toilet is up there in the number one place for me. While you can always go out in your backyard and dig a hole to dispose of your sewage (if you happen to have a backyard, that is), considering American modesty, the smell, and the inconvenience, this quickly becomes an intolerable situation.

A portable toilet costs only about $70 (1981), doesn't take up too much room, conserves water, and is clean and easy to use. It consists basically of two tanks and a toilet bowl with a seat. One tank holds fresh water, which is used for flushing with a small hand or foot pump. The other tank contains the disinfectant chemicals and raw sewage. The chemicals include a powerful deodorizer which works pretty well. There is a hand-operated valve between the bowl and the second reservoir. If you control a tendency to use lots of flushing water, you will have to empty the sewage only once every three or four days and use only two gallons of fresh water for flushing. A family of two will get thirty or forty uses before the tank fills up.

While we are on this subject of portable toilets, let me offer you some hard-earned advice. The holding tanks of these toilets are airtight, and can generate a lot of pressure, especially when you are sitting on them. Opening the valve under these circumstances guarantees a most unwelcome eruption of sewage from the bowl which splashes several feet in the air. To avoid this experience, always open the valve to release the pressure *before* using the toilet, and open the valve again to flush the bowl only *after* standing up and putting the lid down.

I am adamant on the subject of using portable toilets because of my experience during our family's Three-Day Test. We had planned to flush the bathroom toilet once a day using the waste water from doing dishes, brushing teeth, shaving, and personal bathing. At the end of the first day, we were very eager to flush the toilet. The odor was overwhelming. To our amazement, we discovered that it took *all* of our accumulated waste water and an additional two gallons of our emergency drinking water to fill up the toilet's tank enough for a single flush. That was too great a waste of water to consider using in a survival situation, especially in the great Los Angeles desert. We later learned that we could have made the toilet flush with less water if we had poured the water suddenly into the bowl itself rather than pouring it into the tank first.

I recommend that you invest in the chemical disinfectant and the special toilet paper which are offered as accessories for these toilets. We economized, and found that regular toilet paper did not dissolve in the holding tank, which made it much more difficult to empty. It splashed a lot when we poured it out. Ugh! You don't need that kind of problem. Buy the proper accessories.

The subject of sanitation includes much more than just toilet facilities. There are many items we use each day that we never give a thought to. Make it a practice to keep spares of all the following items; then if you run out, you will have them on hand. Be sure to replace them as you use them. If there comes a time when you can't go to the store anymore, you will be very grateful that you thought ahead.

Emergency Sanitary Supplies

Shampoo
Toothpaste
Toothbrushes (enough for guests)
Mouthwash
Soap
Deodorant
Dishwashing detergent
Toilet paper
Tissues
Paper towels

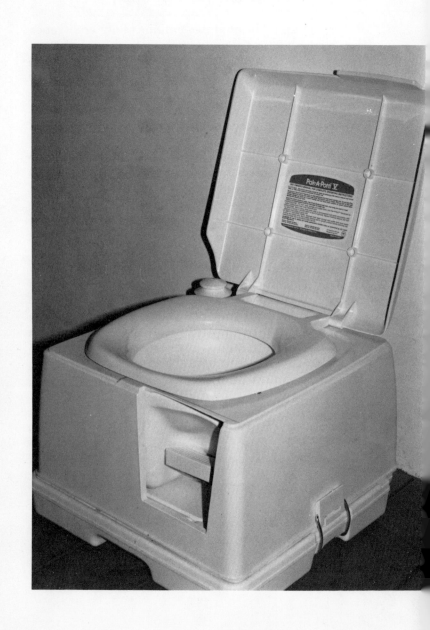

The portable toilet (*left*) is one of civilization's greatest inventions, second only to the nonportable type. It provides the comforts of home when sanitation and water services don't. There are certain items (*below*) we don't think about until we run out of them and can't get more from the store. Better stock up.

Razor blades
Laundry soap
Cotton swabs
Feminine hygiene supplies
Disposable diapers
Plastic garbage bags
Bottle of bleach (for disinfecting diapers)

Incidentally, if you have to do laundry without benefit of your washing machine, you can do a load most quickly by using the bathtub. Toss the clothes into the tub and add just enough water to cover them. Put in the appropriate amounts of soap and bleach, and then agitate the clothes with a plumber's plunger, the big rubber suction cup on a stick usually used for unplugging drains. Pushing the plunger down against the clothes forces water through them, which is especially helpful with soiled diapers. Drain, rinse, and wring.

The last problem concerning sanitation is garbage. I don't have the statistic on how much garbage Americans produce, but it must be staggering. We live in a rural area with a small population, but almost every time we go to the dump, the dumping area has been filled and moved to a different location. If garbage becomes a problem, the best bet is to burn all of it, then rake the unburnable cans and foil wrappers out of the ashes. Smash the cans flat and bury or store the residue outside in heavy plastic bags. If you have burned the cans in a hot fire, they will be clean, dry, and not attractive to animals. Garbage accumulates quickly (especially if you are depending on canned foods), and you will be glad that you are not tripping over open grocery bags full of smelly cans.

5. Please Don't Take My Sunshine Away

The topics of emergency lighting, heating, and cooking naturally go together. In most American homes, when the commercial utilities fail, families instantly lose their lights, and then discover that their thermostats don't work either. Then around dinner time they find out that nothing is colder than an electric range in a blackout. There isn't much that's warmer than a thawing freezer either. So what kind of preparations can you make to meet these challenges when the power fails? We'll look at devices for emergency lighting, cooking, and heating. As for refrigeration, well, we're working on it.

Lights

We really take the electric light bulb for granted. Witness the number of people in our society who are night people. They sleep until noon and function best after eight in the evening. This would not be possible without artificial light. I happen to be one of the more light-oriented types, up at six and to bed by ten. But I, too, was greatly affected by the changes of the light cycle during our first Three-Day Test.

When the lights go out, you are stuck in the dark, and there are no two ways about it. The first thing you look for is some artificial light. What kind depends on what you have available and how comfortable you are with it depends on how prepared you were.

The first thing you need is a flashlight, preferably one with a big battery. One with two or three C batteries isn't going to hold up if you need it for three weeks. The flashlight can give you the means with which to find your other lights in the dark. It is perfect for going outside to check out that strange noise, and you can easily take it to a part of the house that is dark.

Just as important as having the flashlight is knowing where it is when the lights go out. If it is hidden in an obscure drawer at the far end of the house, it won't do you any good. Keep it in some definite place, and keep it there all the time except when you are using it. We keep our flashlight in the bedroom, which is the only part of the house we really know our way around in the dark.

Also, store several extra batteries in your refrigerator. They will keep a lot longer in the refrigerator than they will in a drawer somewhere. It's nice to have a set of spare bulbs, too. In fact, that's why we prefer battery flashlights to the hand-powered kind. We could never find a replacement bulb for our novelty flashlight with the built-in generator.

One flashlight we do like is called MoonLight, manufactured by Early Winters (110 Prefontaine Place South, Seattle, WA 98104). It costs $20 (1980), expensive for a pocket flashlight, but it has some unique features. This squat little flashlight is about five inches long and one and a half inches in diameter. It is made of clear lexan plastic (like motorcycle helmet faceplates) and is completely watertight. It runs on a single lithium cell with a usable life of over twelve hours and a shelf life of between six and ten *years*. It also contains its own set of three spare bulbs. There is a band of material inside which glows in the dark so you can find the light when

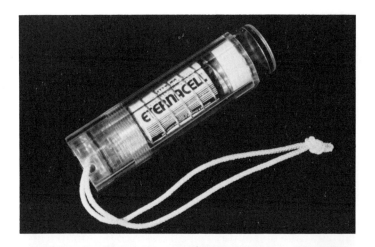

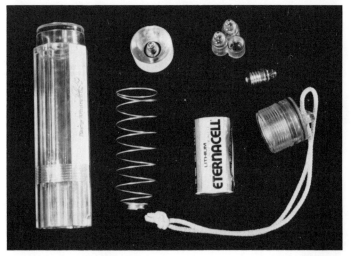

The Moonlight from Early Winters (*top*) is a unique emergency flashlight. It glows in the dark so you can find it when the power fails, and is simple, waterproof, and unbreakable. Included is a lithium battery with a 10-year shelf life and three extra bulbs (*bottom*).

you need it. We have a spare battery for ours in the refrigerator. About 1990 or so, we'll let you know how it works.

Once you have given yourself some "instant" light, it is time to think about longer-term light. Candles are a great standby, with some very distinctive advantages and disadvantages. They are relatively inexpensive and easily available. They are safe to store and can be operated without instructions. However, candles can be very misleading too. Many decorative and dinner candles will last a total of about three hours if you burn them continually. They also have a tendency to drip hot wax on your hand—or carpet—so you need a container under them to hold the melted wax. They are also very hazardous and may start fires, especially if you are clumsy (like me) or have small children (again like me).

Last, but certainly not least, the main problem with candles is the quality of the light they radiate: it is very poor. If you want romance, you should light a candle, but if you want to read, forget it. If you have a single candle in the bathroom, you'll be able to use the toilet without difficulty, but any activity which requires more light than that is going to be difficult to perform with only candlelight. That's why candelabras were so popular in the Middle Ages. If you want to see anything, you'll need at least four or five candles just for a start.

Candles do have their place, though, and it's a good idea to have a few on hand. We use stick candles ten inches high and two inches thick. They burn slowly which is an important consideration. Experiment with one or two samples before you buy several because they are big and look like they ought to burn a long time. Some of these candles will be finished in an hour. Beware of the "survival candles" which come in metal cans, too. They do burn fifty to seventy-five hours as advertised, but they give off very little light and the deeper the candle burns into the can, the dimmer the light since the can itself shades the candle.

The next step we took in search of light was to try some kerosene wick lamps. These are the five-dollar kerosene lamps you see in the grocery stores from time to time. When we were just starting out, we bought several of these lamps, a few quarts of lamp oil, and thought we had it made. Guess again. It turns out that there is an art to using kerosene lamps—their selection, care, feeding, and placement around the house—which we learned little by little.

The very first thing we discovered during our first Three-Day Test was that these lamps shed a useful amount of light, up to a point. You can even read by them if you place the book on a table with a lamp on both sides. What's a little eyestrain in a survival situation, right? But when we had to take the baby into the next room to change his pants, we quickly discovered that while the kerosene lamps we had purchased might be decorative, we couldn't pick one up with one hand because the base was too wide to grip, especially with a little spilled lamp oil clinging to the glass. So it was back to the store for lamps we could grasp. When you shop for lamps, make sure you take into account that they will be full of liquid during use, making them heavier and more awkward. Also try to find lamps with snug-fitting glass chimneys. Loose chimneys have a tendency to fall off.

We also purchased a kerosene lamp designed to hang on the wall which saves looking for a shelf or other safe place to put it. You only need a wall and a nail. Also, since it hangs high, it sheds its light over a greater area. It is out of the way from the exploring hands of children and accidental bumping. By driving nails in several

Our first experiment with kerosene lamps was disappointing. Wick lamps (*below*) are best for mood lighting. The lamp on the left hangs on a wall. Beware of lamps like the center one which cannot be easily held in one hand. Aladdin kerosene lamps (*right*) are utilitarian since they are as bright as electric lights, and can be converted to electricity.

locations, you can carry the lamp from one spot to another as you move around the house.

So with three or four strategically located kerosene lamps, some of which were easily carried, we got along quite nicely. It was then that we made a quantum jump in our sophistication: we discovered the Aladdin mantle lamps. These lamps are quite expensive with the cheapest running about $40 (1981), but they will light up a whole room almost as well as electric lights. In fact, when we first got our mantle lamps, I wasn't home. When I walked in that evening, I didn't notice that Bruce had turned the electricity off, even though the only light in the house was coming from these lamps. That's bright! In addition to giving off between eight and ten times more light than the regular kerosene lamps, the mantle lamps also give off quite a bit of heat. Two mantle lamps burning in our medium-sized living room made it unnecessary for us to have a fire on cool winter nights. If you don't like the idea of having all these kerosene lamps cluttering up your house, there are electric conversion kits available, too. The lamp can be electric until the electricity goes out, and then can be converted to kerosene. Many of the Aladdin lamps are very pretty, too. What could be better? You should keep some spare mantles (which are very fragile) and wicks (which get used up) on hand to keep your lamps in shape.

The main difficulty in using kerosene lamps is storing the kerosene. The mantle lamps also use kerosene, as opposed to commercial lamp oil which has so much residue it blackens the mantles. Kerosene isn't particularly flammable, but you must take some precautions. We tested kerosene's flammability by dropping a lighted match into a bowl of kerosene and the match extinguished itself. However, the safest way to store

The difference between conventional kerosene lamps and
Aladdin lamps is vividly apparent here. The wick lamps are
above, the Aladdins below. Which would you rather work
with?

your kerosene is still to keep it in an Explosafe can. These are five-gallon gasoline cans which cost about thirty dollars at the hardware store. They are designed to prevent the explosion of flammable liquids. Store your fuel in a well-ventilated outbuilding to prevent fire hazard. You will have problems with fumes if your container isn't airtight.

How much kerosene you store depends on what kind of lamps you are using, how many of them you have, and how long you are planning on using them. The rule of thumb is that the regular kerosene lamps use a cup of fuel in six hours, and the mantle lamps use a cup of fuel in about three hours. You will need many more regular lamps than mantle lamps to make equal light, though, so don't forget to add this into your calculations. You will probably need the lamps no longer than four hours per night. If you use two mantle lamps for four hours a night for a month, you will need to store about five gallons of kerosene.

The best kerosene for the Aladdin lamps is Chevron (Standard) pearl grade kerosene. You may have to call several dealers before you find one who will sell you only five gallons, though. They have to buy it in fifty-five-gallon drums.

Temperature Control

We Americans have learned how to control our environment to a very great degree. We use air conditioning when it is too hot, and heating when it is too cold. If it is too dark, we turn on the lights, and if it is too bright, we close the curtains. The ability to adapt our environment to suit ourselves has made our lives a lot more comfortable than they were only a few decades ago, and I, for one, have come to take it for granted. Yet I know that is a dangerous attitude.

For storing liquid fuels, an Explosafe can is good (*top*) but a dry-chemical extinguisher is handy. A match burns itself out in a pool of kerosene on the left (*bottom*), while a pan of Coleman fuel (white gasoline) flames when lit.

[URBAN ALERT!]

We recently moved to the Sierra Nevadas where we experience hot summers and cold winters in contrast to the two years we spent in Los Angeles where it is spring-like all year. But with the air conditioning and heating in our homes, cars, and stores we visit, we are really spending almost all our time in the most comfortable environment possible. The problem comes when these amenities are no longer available to us. We have no tolerance for even fairly minor variations in temperatures.

I think that as a nation, we have made some real progress in this area in the last few years. With rising energy costs, people have become more conscious of thermostatic settings. We have relearned things which were once common-sense knowledge. One of the very best ways of adapting to temperature variations is wearing clothes suited to the environment. If it is too hot, wear shorts and light, sleeveless shirts. If it gets cold where you live, make sure you have the clothes to keep you warm. When we were living in Montana, we had full-length thermal underwear, warm socks, boots, hats, mufflers, gloves, and heavy jackets. This is not the desired attire for detail work, but it sure beats being cold. Of course, if you are staying in the house, a layer of blankets or a bundlebag will do nicely. If you are ever really in danger of freezing, you can always rip up the carpets and use them as thick, warm, but dusty, blankets.

Let me tell you a story about how fast conventional houses lose their heat. My husband and I were living in a big, drafty, old house one cold winter in Montana. The temperature was about ten degrees one early Saturday morning, when we discovered that the furnace would not stay lit. It would heat the house fine, but when it turned off, the pilot light would extinguish and Bruce

[48]

had to go outside to the basement to relight it. Since it is impossible to get a repairman on weekends, we settled in for a couple of cold days. The house would go from seventy to forty degrees in about four hours, so even though we went to bed late at night, by the next morning, it was icy inside. We spent the weekend dressed like Eskimos and shivering under the covers. This was only an intermittent problem for us for one weekend, but it sure taught me the importance of being prepared.

Clothing is probably the easiest, but also the least effective, means of controlling your environment. The ideal way of keeping warm when the furnace doesn't work is to have an energy-efficient wood-burning stove or fireplace. If you are lucky enough to have one, all you have to do is stock up on wood and matches and get a little practice starting fires without using a lot of newspapers. We have learned how to bank a fire at night so there are some coals to build up the fire again in the morning without much work. It takes a lot of time to chop wood, and a fire must be tended several times during the day, but it is very satisfying work. (But Bruce grumbles, "She doesn't split the wood.")

If you don't have a fireplace or wood stove and aren't in a position to get one, you can still get a portable heater. There are white gas and kerosene heaters commercially available. Our kerosene heater is one of Survival, Inc.'s better quality cooker-heaters and looks a little like a kerosene lamp grown to the size of a wastebasket. It has been disappointing to use as a cooker since it takes thirty minutes to boil a quart of water, but it really warms up a room. It consumes eight ounces of kerosene in one hour.

There isn't much to say about cooling. Unfortunately there aren't any nifty devices to keep you cool when the electricity fails in the summer unless you want to buy a propane refrigerator, which is probably more preparation than you had in mind. Bruce says that when he was a little boy in Missouri, his mother used to wet their sheets with water to cool them off at night when the temperature was still over a hundred degrees and the humidity was 90 percent. They used electric fans, of course, but don't forget that you can make hand fans to help keep you cool when the electric ones don't work.

Cooking

Just before writing this book, we had an opportunity to test several kinds of emergency cook stoves. If you are thinking about economizing by not buying a stove, just open a can of chili and eat it cold, grease and all. Could you stand a week of that? Three weeks?

We tested a two-burner Coleman stove, a propane stove, a Mountain Safety Research (MSR) camp stove, and a little wood stove designed for backpackers called a Zip Ztove. The results of these tests and fuel consumption figures are given below.

We tend to rely on our Coleman camp stove model 425 which has two burners, runs on white gas, and is about the size of a small suitcase. It is inexpensive at $19.95 (1980) and very efficient. It boils a quart of water in five and a half minutes on its main burner and uses seven and a half ounces of gas in an hour. On the secondary burner, it takes ten and a half minutes to boil the water, and with both burners going, it consumes a total of eleven ounces of fuel per hour.

The main problem with the Coleman stove is that you have to store white gas, which is dangerously flammable, much more so than kerosene. You also have to keep pumping the fuel tank to keep the pressure up, and if you cook on the stove for several days, the pumping makes for a sore thumb. But other than that, the

Our wood stove heats the house while it keeps water and soup simmering. We have two cords of wood seasoning for the winter.

The Coleman camp stove (*top*) is a well-known outdoor stove and is available at sporting goods stores for a modest price. The Coleman oven (*bottom*) sits on top of the stove and is a handy addition.

Coleman stove is very satisfactory and reasonably convenient.

Coleman also sells an oven which sits on top of most of the larger two-burner camp stoves. Basically, the oven is a box which traps the heat from one burner, and folds up neatly into a small package for storage. We experimented with our oven and had satisfactory results, although it took some practice. The thermometer on the front door of ours was totally inaccurate, and we found that the oven must be exactly centered over the burner for any semblance of even cooking. But we successfully baked sweet rolls from raw dough one morning during our Three-Day Test. This is the only way we know to bake raised breads in an emergency situation.

The second stove we tested was a Sears model 672764 two-burner propane camp stove which cost $40 (1981). It is very similar to the Coleman stove, but is fueled by a sealed propane cylinder about the size of a one-pound coffee can. This stove is the easiest to use of the stoves we tested. Because the fuel is already under pressure, you have only to turn a knob and light it. It works very much like a regular stove and storing the propane cans is quite a bit safer than keeping tins of gasoline around. However, the canisters cost $2.19 (1981) for about eighteen ounces of fuel, which is only enough for two to three hours of cooking. The stove boils a quart of water in six and a half minutes (just one minute longer than the Coleman), and uses only six ounces of fuel in an hour (whereas the Coleman uses seven and a half ounces). With both burners on, the stove uses about nine ounces of fuel per hour.

We discovered a very special advantage in using the propane stove. We did our Three-Day Test in June, when it was very hot here in the foothills. With no refrigeration or cold streams nearby, we were without anything cold. As the propane canister provides heat for the stove, it becomes quite cold to the touch. Frost forms on the sides of the canister. We found that by setting the canister in a bowl of fruit salad while our dinner was cooking, not only did we cook our dinner, but we cooled our dessert. How's that for energy efficient?

After testing the camp stoves, we tried out two back-packing stoves. The first was the MSR backpack stove. This little stove consists of a small burner connected by a ten-inch-long fuel line to an aluminum fuel bottle. It is available in many backpacking stores, but can also be obtained by writing to Eastern Mountain Sports (Vose Farm Road, Peterborough, NH 03458). It is one of the most expensive stoves we tested, costing $74.50 plus $6.00 for the Sigg bottle (1981), but it also has one advantage over all the others. It can use any of about a half-dozen different fuels, including white gas, kerosene, diesel, and leaded gas. This is a very important consideration if you have to scrounge for fuel. There have even been reports of running the MSR stove on fermented papaya juice!

We tested it with kerosene and white gas. With white gas, the MSR stove boils a quart of water in five and a half minutes when used with a windscreen and uses only six and a half ounces of fuel in an hour. When used with kerosene, the water takes one minute longer to boil, but consumes only four ounces of fuel in an hour. This is very efficient. The major disadvantage to this stove is also its reason for existence. It is a very small and lightweight stove designed for efficient backpacking use. However, the burner is only three inches across and pans rest fairly precariously on it. It doesn't provide the wide grating that larger camp stoves do.

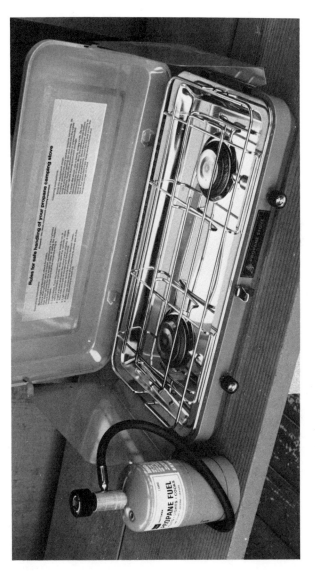

Propane camp stoves, like this one from Sears, are easy and safe for home use. Attach the fuel canister, then use it as you would a gas range. The canister eliminates handling and storing dangerous fuels.

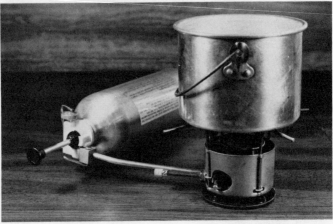

The tiny Zip Ztove (*top*) boils water in four minutes. Its battery-powered blower creates a roaring, sooty fire that burns anything. The MSR stove (*bottom*) is a safe stove and burns a variety of fuels.

The last stove we tried out was the little Zip Ztove, which is a wood-burning backpacker stove. It has a small fire chamber which is fanned by an electric motor run from a C cell battery. You can burn sticks, kindling, pine cones, or almost anything, and the motor will fan the flames into a roaring fire. One foot of broom handle, chopped into small pieces, is enough fuel to boil a quart of water in four and a half minutes, which is very impressive. The only problem is that it blackens the pot badly and is so smoky that there is just no way to use it inside the house. You have to remember to store extra batteries, too. But the nice thing is what you *don't* have to store—white gas, propane, or kerosene. The Zip Ztove costs $21.95 and is made by Z. Z. Corp., (10806 Kaylor St., Los Alamitos, CA 90720).

So these were the stoves we tested. Each has pros and cons and you must decide for yourself which you want to buy, and what kind and how much fuel you want to store. Remember that you will be heating water for washing, doing dishes, preparing meals, and taking sponge baths, so make sure you have enough fuel. Having the proper equipment and then running out of fuel would be very frustrating.

There are three other things to remember when it comes to cooking and stoves. Make sure you have a supply of heavy-duty wooden kitchen matches. You will be glad you do. Secondly, you must *always maintain adequate ventilation* when using any of these stoves. Even if it is very cold outside, you must open a window, or you may solve all of your survival problems permanently. These stoves can use all your oxygen and leave you trying to breathe carbon monoxide. Be careful. Thirdly, it is wise to have a chemical fire extinguisher by your side when you are using these stoves. We were very glad we did when our stove overheated in our first

Three-Day Test. Get a good-sized extinguisher rated for liquid fuel fires. My husband recently joined the volunteer fire department and after an exercise in which he was asked to put out a pan of flaming fuel with a fire hose, he rushed to the store to buy two of the big all-purpose chemical extinguishers. It doesn't take much to make a believer out of you when you squirt water into a flaming bucket and the fire just keeps burning. Get those extinguishers.

Utensils

We learned a lot about what kind of utensils to have on hand during our successful Three-Day Test. I had some paper plates, bowls, and cups on hand, figuring the fewer dishes I had to do, the more water I could conserve. That was very true, but then there was the trade-off in the amount of garbage we accumulated. Disposables create an inordinate amount of trash in a short period of time. But if you have licked the problem of what to do with your trash, and won't be without services for a very long time, they are certainly the easiest way to go. After our test, I decided to buy a few disposable pots and pans of the tinfoil variety. I didn't find exactly what I was looking for, but foil pans and pie plates will do in a pinch.

We also found we needed at least two pitchers for pouring water. A five-gallon jerry can is a little awkward when you are trying to brush your teeth. We also made almost continuous use of two medium-sized saucepans for heating water. Make very sure that whatever you use to pour water, you keep very clean. Don't let your sanitary standards relax just because it may be easier to use a community cup dipped into the kettle. Give everyone a separate cup and make them pour the water into it, not dip it into the water. This is not the time to get sick.

For short-term survival, disposable plates, cups, utensils and pans eliminate having to wash dishes and save water. Two pots and two pitchers are used for heating and carrying water.

6. An Apple a Day

An apple a day is supposed to keep the doctor away, but the real problem comes when you need the doctor and can't get him. Getting adequate medical attention is a tough subject to deal with. We are not doctors, and each of us has a greater or lesser understanding of what medicine is all about. I cannot give you a short course here on how to doctor yourself, so instead I will recommend a few books and a list of supplies you should purchase.

There are a lot of good first-aid and health books on the market these days, and reading them will give you a much better understanding of your body and how it works. I will briefly mention three books that are good for general purposes, and two books that are extremely helpful in an emergency where a doctor is not available.

The first book is *A Sigh of Relief,* produced by Martin I. Green (Bantam 01155-3, 1977, $7.95). This is a first-aid handbook for handling children's emergencies and is designed for use by panicky parents. It has large, clear pictures and an easy-to-use index. The emergency section deals with such problems as bites, stings, bleeding, broken bones, artificial respiration, burns, choking, drowning, eye injuries, fever, poisoning, shock, sprains, and much more. It also contains an excellent section on how to childproof your house and garage areas, and on safety precautions in hiking, bike riding, cars, and toys. If you have children in your home or visiting, don't be without this book.

The second book you shouldn't be without is *How To Be Your Own Doctor (Sometimes)* by Dr. Keith Sehnert with Howard Eisenberg (Grosset & Dunlap 14466, 1975, $5.95). My husband and I heard Dr. Sehnert speak at a conference once and were fascinated. He contends that most visits to the doctor are unnecessary, and discusses which conditions he thinks require a doctor's attention and which do not. He tells you what symptoms to be on the lookout for and what information you should have ready before you call the doctor. He also advocates the patient becoming an active partner with the doctor in his or her own health care and provides a list of over-the-counter and prescription medicines to have on hand. I highly recommend that you not only buy the book, but that you also read it before you need it.

To go along with medical self-help books, I recommend getting a Marshall Black Bag Kit which includes a blood pressure kit, stethoscope, otoscope (for looking in ears), dental reflector, tongue depressor, oral and rectal thermometers, and a high-intensity examination flashlight. In addition the kit contains Sehnert's *The Self-Help Medical Guide* (which is also part of Sehnert's book), a *Self-Instruction Program* for learning how to use the instruments, and various forms for recording your family's health history. This excellent kit of valuable equipment sells at Survival Inc. for $120 (1981). The only problem with it is that it contains no bandages, but we'll come to that.

My nomination for the best buy in health books is *Family Health and Home Nursing* by the American Red Cross (Doubleday, 1979, $2.95). This book has 600 information-filled pages that take you from pregnancy

to death and everything in between. This is a textbook
for nurses, and covers the details of home medical care
not usually covered in books written for doctors. Changing a sheet with the patient still in the bed is something
the doctor isn't necessarily expected to know how to do.
There are sections on how to stay well, home nursing
care, detecting illnesses, first aid at home, improvising
equipment, and natural disasters. It is the kind of book
you should read for general information which might be
vitally helpful to you someday. You certainly can't beat
the price.

The fourth book I recommend to you is of a totally
different nature. It is called *Where There Is No Doctor,
A Village Health Care Handbook* by David Werner
(Paladin Press, P.O. Box 1307, Boulder, CO 80306, 1977,
$14.95). This book was designed for use by remote vil-
lagers in Latin America who don't have medical care
available and don't read very well. There are many
step-by-step illustrations and the instructions are very
simply and clearly written. There is some emphasis on
diseases which sanitary conditions have pretty much
eliminated in the United States, but in a stressful situation, some of these problems may reappear. Remember
the garbage strike in New York City? It also tells about
emergency first aid and how to deliver a baby, in addition to describing a valuable medical kit for home supplies. It is a very worthwhile book.

By far the most comprehensive book on emergency
medical self-help is put out by the U.S. Public Health
Service, called *The Ship's Medicine Chest and Medical
Aid at Sea* (1978 edition, U.S. Govt. Printing Office
Stock No. 017-029-00026-6, $18.00). It is designed for
caring for seamen who are too far from port to receive
immediate medical attention in case of accident or

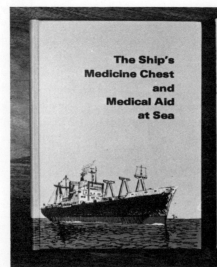

The Ship's
Medicine Chest
and
Medical Aid
at Sea

A Sigh of Relief

the first-aid
handbook
for
childhood
emergencies

Produced by Martin I. Green

Preface by Vincent L. Tofany,
President of the National Safety Council
Introduction by Kenneth Jay Solomon, M.D.

THE ONLY BOOK OF ITS KIND
★ Fast, simple instructions for every childhood injury and illness.
★ Hundreds of step-by-step illustrations.
★ How to prevent accidents from happening.

WHERE THERE IS NO DOCTOR
a village health care handbook
David Werner

Family
Health
and Home
Nursing

American
Red Cross

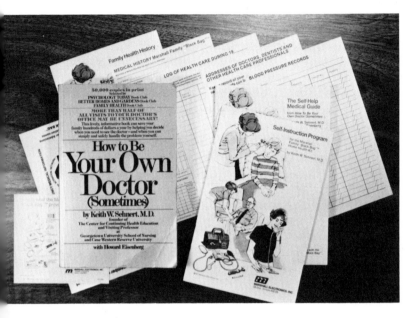

The Ship's Medicine Chest (*top, left*) is the best book for medical self-help. *A Sigh of Relief* has an index and self-explanatory drawings. *Where There Is No Doctor* (*bottom, left*) is a guide to getting along without medical services. *Family Health and Home Nursing* is the Red Cross text for nurses. *How To Be Your Own Doctor* (*Sometimes*) (*top*) is an excellent self-help manual. The Marshall Black Bag first-aid kit was designed for use with this book and includes a self-instruction guide for using the instruments.

illness. It is an extremely comprehensive book that even shows how to suture and give injections.

Each of the books I am recommending has its own list of over-the-counter medications and prescription drugs you should stock. I suggest you look at the books, find those that suit you the best, then follow their recommendations on what to have on hand. Having the medicines with no book to tell you how to use them will do you no good.

If you are doubtful about obtaining the prescription drugs, let me tell you about our experience. We recently moved into a small town where we didn't know anyone. We made an appointment with a local doctor and explained why we wanted the drugs. The doctor was very receptive and immediately gave us prescriptions for the items we requested. As long as you demonstrate that you are reasonable, responsible, and will not use the drugs except in an emergency, you should have no problem. While you are at it, remember to ask for additional prescriptions of medications you take regularly so you do not get in a bind if they suddenly become unavailable. Make sure you look at the expiration date on these medicines and get them refilled, so you are not left in an emergency with outdated supplies. Take the unused medicines back to your doctor when you ask for your refills to show him that you took good care of them.

When Bruce was writing *Life After Doomsday,* he spent quite a bit of time searching for emergency dental information, but found almost nothing. Three years later we are in a better situation. Survival Inc. is offering an excellent dental kit for only $20 (1981). This kit will let you make minor repairs to loose fillings, caps, and bridges, as well as administer first aid for broken teeth. The kit contains oil of cloves to deaden the pain, temporary filling material, dental wax, various instru-

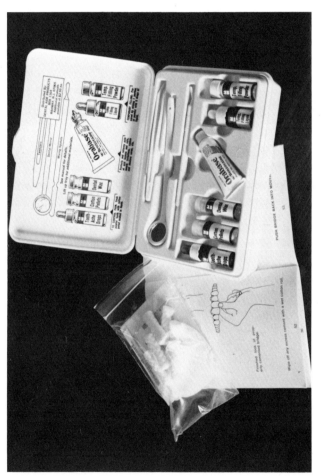

Most people don't even know that dental first-aid kits exist. A kit like this one will be most welcome when you can't get to the dentist during a blizzard.

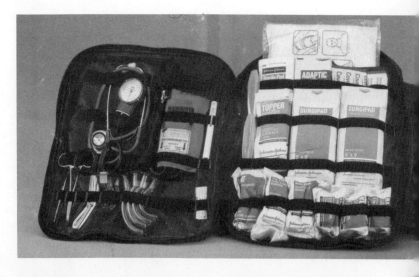

The Rescue Services Pac (*top*) is one of the best first-aid kits. It folds into a soft-sided suitcase or backpack and unfolded contains a full selection of paramedical equipment and supplies. At $195, it is worth the price. These medical supplies fit into one medium-sized cardboard box (*bottom*). The kit contains prescription medicines and also over-the-counter medicines we'd be hard-pressed to do without.

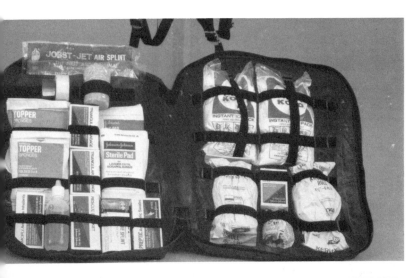

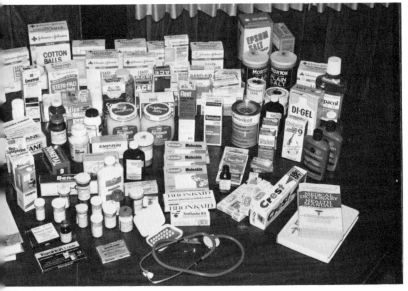

ments, and a very helpful and clearly illustrated instruction manual. If you have ever had a loose filling over the weekend, you'll understand why we recommend buying this kit.

If you are ready to become actively involved in your own health care, there are a few more things you can do. Every community offers cardiopulmonary resuscitation (CPR) and first-aid courses at almost no cost. Call your Red Cross office to check on their availability in your area. Spend the few evenings it will take to learn the material and build your confidence in your ability to handle an emergency situation. Someday you may be very glad you did.

We have spent several years looking for a good first-aid kit, and I am pleased to tell you that we have recently found one. Most preassembled first-aid kits cost about three times what it would cost to put the components together yourself and contain so little material that they are practically worthless. In desperation we finally went out to our discount drug store and purchased about fifty dollars' worth of bandages and first-aid supplies which was enough to fill a large carton.

Though we knew this was not a complete kit, we thought that at least we had made a substantial start. Then at Easter our two-year-old son burned his arm on our wood stove. It was a classic second-degree burn about the size of a quarter, and I was very glad we had some bandages around. After soaking his arm in cold water for half an hour, we wrapped his burn in a gauze bandage which covered his entire forearm. Little children are very active and we found that we had to replace the bandage several times a day in order to keep the burned area covered and clean. After three days our supply of gauze was exhausted and our local drug store had only one roll of gauze in stock. This taught us the lesson of what a tremendous amount of bandaging material is required for even a minor injury, and how little we can depend on outside sources to have what we need in an emergency. Imagine what it would be like if everybody in town needed that one box of gauze!

This summer we were contacted by Rescue Services, Inc. (P.O. Box 16, Auburn, CA 95603) about their new Rescue Services Pac designed for use by paramedics and rescue personnel. The equipment is contained in a heavy-duty orange nylon backpack which also has a grip handle. The many useful items in this handy pack are easily accessible and visible and include inflatable splints and instant cold packs, in addition to a wide variety of bandages (several of each type). We decided that this was the first-aid kit we had been looking for and immediately purchased it. It cost $195 (1981) plus tax, or $160 without the stethoscope and blood pressure kit. After we had bought bandages individually for as much as $3.95 for six bandages, we thought this kit was a bargain. Rescue Services also sells first-aid refills by mail, and their supply list is very impressive.

7. What to Do When There's Nothing to Do

It's hard to predict what the worst psychological problem faced by disaster victims is likely to be. Riot-zone residents endure the rioting in constant fear. Tornado, earthquake, and wildfire victims who have lost their homes suffer from disorientation, shock, and sorrow. People who have lost loved ones, of course, are primarily occupied with grief. Victims whose survival depends on constant effort, such as people clinging to rooftops in a flood, seldom have the leisure to develop emotional problems at the time.

But one of the most common psychological problems encountered by survivors, especially people in fallout shelters, is simply boredom. Our society is so geared to going places and doing things, largely through the indiscriminate use of gasoline and electricity, that when we are cut off from our normal activities, we don't know what to do. Just ask parents with a lot of children and a broken TV set. "Mommy, I don't have anything to do!" is what they hear. This really came home to me during our Three-Day Test. Fortunately, my family reads for recreation (even the two-year-old after a fashion), but after a full day of lying around reading, we got pretty restless.

The psychological side of preparedness is usually entirely overlooked. I'm not old enough to tell you what we did in "the good old days" before TV, so I'll just offer some suggestions. It's important for each member of the family to keep busy during a crisis and feel they are being useful, so each one should be involved as fully as possible in daily survival activities. Whenever you get a chance, make a big production of anything that needs to be done. We have become a society of fast-food restaurants, of which I am a great fan, but during emergencies make a family activity of preparing each meal. There's the project of deciding what to eat, setting the table, cooking the meal, and cleaning up after-wards. Since you may be eating outside, even the youngest members of the family can be occupied with such obviously important duties as shooing away flies from the food and chasing paper plates that have blown off the table. You may not have much control over the flies, but you can restrain yourself from weighting down the plates!

Every family member can help with some aspect of the operation of eating, and since it occurs three times a day, it takes up a lot of "free" time. Just ask any mother. If there is any conflict about who does what job, rotate the jobs every meal so everyone gets a chance to see how hard the other guy has it.

Books and Reading

Now, what do you do for the other twelve hours of the day? If your family reads, you are ahead of the game. You will not only have plenty of time for quietly reading those books you never got around to (circumstances permitting), but you will also be transported away from your troubles, even if only for a little while. In addition to reading to yourself, you can take turns with your family in reading books aloud. You can also each talk about your favorite book, and why it is your favorite.

[74]

Lively and informative books and games help prevent boredom when usual forms of entertainment aren't available.
Some offer private escapism, others promote family discussion. If you have little children, include games for them.

Not only will you get some lively discussions going, you may also discover yourself growing closer to your family than ever before.

If reading is not one of your family's main sources of entertainment, let me suggest a few books you might want to buy and have on hand if you are ever stuck for something to do. Books like the *Guiness Book of World Records* and *The Book of Lists* are very entertaining and you will learn all kinds of interesting trivia. These books also contain a lot of information on the world's greatest disasters, which may be of interest under the circumstances.

Conversation

Communication is a skill we must continually practice or we get rusty at it. Our society currently encourages little practice. This makes for very lonely people. You might find a disaster to be the most meaningful time of your life if you take the time to learn to talk to your family.

One book you should strongly consider buying is the *Encyclopedia of Serendipity* by Lyman Coleman (Serendipity House, Box 1012, Littleton, CO 80160). It is a group activity book for Bible study groups, but it has some very valuable suggestions even if you are not religiously inclined. There are a lot of communication exercises and icebreaking games to get your family or group going. Once you start sharing your experiences, feelings, and past, you and your family can be left to your own devices for several weeks and actually find yourselves enjoying it!

Talk to each other. Talk about what's happening, and why it is happening. Talk about where each member of the family is heading and how the others can help. Talk about what you want out of life, and how important your family is to you. What starts out as a time of adversity might teach you how to really communicate with those you love. It might be awkward to start with, but persevere because the rewards are worthwhile.

Games and Crafts

There are many people who don't read for enjoyment, and who just can't talk to others without some superficial excuse for keeping the conversation going. For these people, there are games. I decided to see just how many games a typical family might have on hand, and after collecting our own and a few from a neighbor, I covered an entire table with them. As a matter of fact, my husband is a fantasy and war game fan and I decided to leave most of his games out of the picture. We all have games we never have the time or opportunity to play. Make sure you have at least three or four on hand. Don't forget to stock games the children can play, too.

Games for Family Entertainment

Monopoly:	An all-time favorite which really burns up the hours.
Chess:	For the brainy among us.
Checkers:	Very popular, and an easy game to teach children.
Othello:	A very entertaining and unusual game like checkers in some ways.
Dominoes:	Good for groups of adults who must play with children as well as other adults.
Tri-Ominos:	Triangular dominoes that also come with pictures instead of numbers on the pieces for pre-schoolers who want to play too.

Yahtzee:	For folks who like to throw dice.
Card games:	Infinite variations including magic tricks.

Make sure you have a rule book on card games and you can have several weeks of fun learning and becoming skillful at many different games. If you have a war game buff in your family, he or she will be in seventh heaven having a captive audience to play with. Sometimes I think Bruce looks forward to it.

It might be wise to go to your local hobby shop and pick up some kits for different kinds of handicraft. There are needlepoint kits, beadwork kits, model airplane kits, latch hook, speed tufting, metal figure painting, and all kinds of other activities. Pick a few to suit each member of your family and stash them away for a rainy day, possibly a *very* rainy day. Not many people know that in the golden days of civil defense, some public shelters were stocked with lumber and tools so shelterees would be able to occupy themselves by building their own tables and benches while confined underground. At least it was economical.

There are lots of word and story games you can play that need only active imaginations and willing participants to create very enjoyable times. Do you remember the ghost stories told around a fire when you were in summer camp? There are always the old standbys of charades and hangman. Another good game is a continuing story where each person in succession has to get the hero out of the calamity, in the tradition of the *Perils of Pauline.*

And don't forget that everyone needs to be left alone sometimes. So make sure there are times during the day when everyone participates, and times when everyone is allowed to do his or her own thing.

Radios

You will find that one of your main sources of entertainment during an emergency is listening to your battery-powered radio. You may not think of this as entertainment, but if it keeps you interested and occupied while tuning for news programs, it is serving a recreational purpose. Of course, radios are also vital communication links with the surrounding community and in some cases the right preparation in selecting a radio can save your life.

In many disasters, the most immediately felt effect is the interruption of electric and telephone service. Once your TV doesn't work and your phones are out, you will begin to feel very isolated. And you will be, too. Then your only available information source is likely to be a radio, so having a good one becomes extremely important. Obviously, we are talking about a battery-powered portable, or at least one which can be plugged into the cigarette lighter of your car. Don't forget the car radio itself. Most small portables can be run for days off a car battery, which you can then recharge in about an hour of running the engine. Just don't drain the battery too much before recharging or you'll be out of power.

There are five types of radio communication that are useful during an emergency, and for the most part, each type requires a different type of radio. You don't need all of them, and may pick and choose one to fit your needs. You may also be able to purchase radios which will give you all, or almost all of these bands together. But beware. The portable radios which do everything, usually don't do anything well. Radios that offer less variety in terms of coverage, frequently perform more effectively in tuning in distant, weak, or overlapping signals.

Weather alert radios like this one from Radio Shack (*right*) automatically turn on when toned by the National Weather Service. Warnings of tornadoes, flash floods, hurricanes, blizzards, and nuclear attack are given on this system.

The whole family can get involved with the short-wave radio, but unsupervised experiments should be discouraged. You wouldn't want your only link with the outside world to be severed because someone ran down the batteries. Shown is a Panasonic RF-2200 multiband shortwave receiver (*left*).

EALISTIC   WEATHERADIO ALERT

WEATHER

MIN •   • MAX
VOLUME

[URBAN ALERT!]

Probably the most important kind of radio for use during floods, hurricanes, and tornadoes is a weather alert radio such as the Radio Shack model. The National Weather Service maintains an extensive network of local radio stations which broadcast nothing but weather information twenty-four hours a day. In emergencies, these stations emit a special signal that automatically activates weather alert radios in the vicinity. When the siren on ours goes off, it is usually a flash flood warning, but in other parts of the country, it could be a tornado warning or an update on the course of a hurricane. A pocket portable weather radio will warn you if you are away from home.

A regular AM-FM radio will keep you in touch with the broadcasts of local officials, but it is not likely to be of very much help if you have any reason to suspect that the authorities are managing the news in what they consider their civic duty to prevent panic. Therefore, what you need is a radio with several shortwave bands, too. You will be able to hear Voice of America, BBC News, Radio Moscow, and other English language news broadcasts from around the world which will at least give you an interesting variety of information, even if you don't believe all of it. In addition to the shortwave broadcasts, you can pick up several of the ham radio bands for less formal information exchanges.

In a local disaster, such as a tornado, the first thing you will want to know is what the police, fire, and other disaster services are doing. The best way to find this out is with a small, battery-powered public service scanner utilizing crystals for your local community services. I don't know a lot about the qualities of different kinds of scanners, but you can readily check into that. They range from eighty to several hundred dollars in price, and offer a very wide range of features and accessories, most of which don't seem very useful. I looked at a fifty-channel programable scanner recently and discovered that after it was programed for the sheriff, highway patrol, and fire department, it still had forty-seven channels vacant. What for? Just make sure that when your electricity goes off, the scanner doesn't. Some are AC only! That's when you need it the most, so make sure you can run it on batteries.

Lastly, if your family members may be separated by a short distance during a disaster and want to be able to keep in touch, you should invest in some five-watt CB radios for your cars. They will carry up to about three miles in open terrain, not as far in the city. Communication between family members can be of great comfort in uncertain times. Even if you do not need the CB for that purpose, you might still want to listen to find out what's happening to the people near you. CBs are really handy if you need help too. Channel 9, for instance, is generally kept clear and monitored for emergency messages. Having quick access to other people when the phones are out is comforting.

I don't want to recommend specific equipment in this chapter, but I should at least tell you about the radio we use. We have a Panasonic HF-2200 eight-band portable shortwave receiver with which we are fairly pleased. It receives AM, FM, and all shortwave frequencies from 3.9 to 28 MHz, including the CB frequencies. Unlike shortwave receivers that only tune in scattered parts of the shortwave band, it receives the entire band. It costs about $160 (1981) and runs on four D cells or AC wall current. It came from Grant Manning at Radio West (2015 S. Escondido Blvd., Escondido, CA 92025), who specializes in shortwave radios for emergencies.

8. Don't Tread on Me

by Bruce D. Clayton, Ph.D.

Mary Ellen has asked me to write this chapter about defensive firearms for the urban or suburban disaster victim in case information on this subject would be useful to you. Please understand that neither she nor I are urging you to buy guns: we feel that is entirely your own decision. If the disaster you envision would cause a severe enough breakdown of social structure to interfere with your local police service, you might feel a little better with a gun around the house. In some parts of Los Angeles, for instance, it takes twenty minutes for the police switchboard to answer an emergency call even under normal circumstances. If rioters or looters were setting fire to a house on your block, twenty minutes might be too long to wait. And if the phones didn't work at all, what then?

Another point I want to make before beginning is that I have no intention of presenting myself as a firearms expert. I have acquired some familiarity with the martial arts and combat firearms in my role as an author of survivalist material and have enjoyed a first-name relationship with several leading weapons experts. This discussion, then, is intended to report on what the experts tend to recommend. I have tempered these recommendations with my own experience and judgments to better fit the needs of someone preparing for short-term emergencies.

[85]

[URBAN ALERT!]

Selecting a Firearm

I am assuming that you live in an urban or suburban dwelling where shooting distances are relatively short, and long-range precision will not be required; that you are preparing for a local emergency which will last from one to six weeks, not for a period of years; that your primary use for the firearm will be the protection of your family and neighbors in the absence of effective police services, not hunting; that you will remain near home during the crisis, not travel long-distances on foot; and finally, that you are a novice shooter who will use the firearm mostly for periodic test firings, not a shooting hobbyist.

With these assumptions, there is little doubt that the best defensive firearm to recommend to a novice is a 12- or 16-gauge shotgun. A staple weapon, the advantages of a shotgun are many. It is low priced, usually between $100 and $300 (1981), and has an almost unique capability for one-shot stopping power. It is easy to operate and relatively easy to aim effectively, as opposed to a pistol. Its intimidating muzzle gives intruders second thoughts. The ready availability of ammunition is an important consideration, as is the fact that shotguns are so common, they can be purchased at practically any sporting goods store. My first recommendation, then, is to buy a 12-gauge shotgun and ten boxes of ammunition which will yield 250 shots for about $110 (1981). For your purposes, the make and model of the shotgun are not overwhelmingly important. Just make sure that the gun fires reliably since some don't work as they come out of the box.

Now that the basic recommendation is out of the way, there are some fine points to consider in selecting a shotgun for personal defense. Although I do not want to

[86]

impose these on you as restrictions, I do feel that you should be aware of them. The following features are commonly regarded favorably.

—A magazine which holds about seven shells. This is considerably more than the usual three shots which are the legal maximum for hunting, and rules out single-shot, double-barreled, and three-shell magazine guns unless you already own one. The alternative is to practice the "fire-one, load-one" system, in which case the magazine size is irrelevant, but this takes skill and practice.

—A barrel which is eighteen to twenty-two inches long. To realize the utility of this recommendation, take a broom into your hallway and pretend that you're pointing a shotgun at someone standing at the far end of the hall. Now try to quickly turn to point the other way. Short barrels are commonly available as "police," "riot," or "slug" (deer shooting) barrels. They are quite legal as long as they are at least eighteen inches long.

—Most riot shotguns are either pump-action or automatic weapons. In the first case, you have to manually pump a round from the magazine to the chamber between shots. With the automatic, however, the gun does this for you, so all you have to do is pull the trigger again to fire another shot. For the urban nonshooter, the automatic is probably the better choice. Not only does it do half of the work for you, but it also tends to make the recoil a little more manageable. Professional exhibition shooters frequently prefer pump guns to automatics. The automatics don't cycle fast enough for these people.

—Most riot shotguns are 12-gauge weapons, but you might decide on a smaller 16-gauge gun if you have doubts about the recoil. To an intruder, the appearance

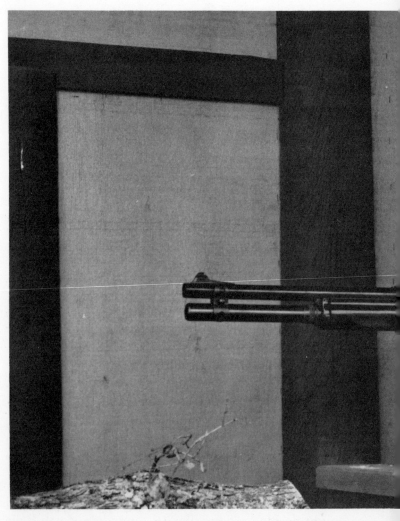

Sometimes a girl's second-best friend is protection. This is a Remingt[...] 870 12-gauge shotgun, slightly modified for home defense. I don't hav[...] lot of interest in guns, but now and then, I'm glad I have this one.

and effects are about the same. Note that I do not recommend the 16-gauge to you, but I think you should be aware of it.

—As for ammunition, there are four recommendations. Usually a salesman will try to sell you 00 buckshot shells for home defense, and they will certainly do the trick although professionals generally prefer #4 buckshot instead. The 00 buckshot shell contains twelve 32-caliber balls while the #4 buckshot shell contains twenty-seven 22-caliber balls. You should also know, however, that garden variety #6 birdshot shells will blow just as big a hole through a man at short range, but the smaller birdshot pellets will be stopped by walls more easily than the heavier buckshot pellets. For indoor and backyard shooting, this avoids the embarrassment of accidentally wounding people on the other side of the house. For greater penetration and range, if that might be necessary, buy slug shells which fire a single lead bullet the size of a marble. You are not necessarily limited to buckshot.

My specific recommendation is a Remington 870 Brushmaster which is a dependable pump shotgun that comes with a twenty-inch barrel. The Remington 1100 is the automatic version, and is very popular in sporting circles. Special combat accessories are made for these guns including magazine extensions (seven shots) and special flashlight holders which attach to the gun to provide light with which to aim the gun at night. See the Survival, Inc. catalog for these accessories.

If the recoil of the shotgun alarms you, in theory or in practice, let me call your attention to the .223 caliber light assault rifles such as the AR-15, AR-180, and especially the Ruger Mini-14, among others. These rifles fire the standard 5.56mm U.S. military cartridge which, although lightweight by military standards, is usually considered adequate for home defense in ranges under 150 yards. These little rifles have almost no recoil at all, use twenty- or thirty-round detachable magazines, shoot one shot every time you pull the trigger, and are very easy to hold and point.

For stay-at-home defense, the Mini-14 probably has the edge due to its ease of operation and its inoffensive appearance. The Mini-14 looks like a toy rifle with a wooden stock, while the others look like machine guns. The Mini-14 is also cheaper than the others. Which one would you rather take home to your dubious relatives?

As for ammunition, under the circumstances envisioned here, six or more spare twenty-round magazines and about five hundred rounds of ammunition would be sufficient. Rioters, arsonists, and other criminals rarely engage in pitched battles. Remember, this is short-term survival we are talking about.

Having discussed shotguns and rifles, I will end with a few comments about handguns. Compared to the long arms, handguns are difficult to use skillfully and most do not have the devastating wounding ability for which shotguns and high-velocity rifles are so justly famous. If you are not skillful with firearms and are considering buying a handgun as your only home defense weapon, I advise you against it. The long guns help you do a better job, and in some cases, you can buy two of them for the price of one pistol. Just ask any policeman what gun he'd chose if he knew he was about to be in a fight. He won't select the .38 caliber handgun he carries in his hip. That's his emergency first-aid kit. For *fighting* he carries a riot shotgun or assault rifle in the patrol car.

If you want to get a pistol in addition to a riotgun or rifle, the common choice is the U.S. military standard .45 caliber Colt autopistol. Combat pistol shooting enthusiasts virtually all use this firearm. On the other hand, revolvers are mechanically simpler than autopistols, and even a totally inexperienced novice can pick one up and shoot it on the first try. There is no slide to pull back and no safety lever to release. In fact, they are so easy for inexperienced people to use that I won't have them around the house. It's your choice, though.

That brings us, however briefly, to the subject of how to keep firearms and children safely under the same roof. Several of our friends have an almost irrational fear of firearms, and turn pale at the thought of a gun in the house with a child. Their fears can be traced largely to their ignorance of firearms.

The standard advice of gun-knowledgeable persons is to acquire a gun cabinet and lock the gun inside it in an unloaded condition. Then take your ammunition and lock it in a separate cabinet somewhere else. Some people go so far as to dismantle the gun and store the pieces in different locked cabinets.

Unfortunately, this makes it impossible to keep a loaded firearm at hand for emergencies because a child or irresponsible adult might get it. How can you resolve this paradox? The key is to strike a balance between the danger of an accidental shooting and the protection a gun offers. You will have to assess the likelihood of criminal attack on your life and the hazard posed by the physical abilities and mischievousness of your child. This is a decision you must make for yourself, knowing that the consequences of error either way could be very serious.

Training

Once you have selected and purchased your firearms, you will need a place to practice with them. For novices, a public shooting range is a good place to learn. To locate such a range, if there isn't one listed in the yellow pages, inquire at your local gun store. If you are truly a novice with firearms, be sure to find someone who can teach you the basics of gun safety before you make your appearance on the range. Otherwise, you could be seriously embarrassed or escorted off the premises.

There are two basic criteria for evaluating your proficiency with firearms. The first is the ability to find the gun, load it, release the safety, fire it, and unload it, all in the dark and without hesitation. When you need a gun in a hurry, it's the wrong time to be reading the instruction manual! Usually, this minimum level of proficiency can be maintained by taking the firearm out once a month or so and refamiliarizing yourself with it, without firing it. Actual, live firing practice each month is preferred, however.

The second criterion of proficiency is whether or not you can hit what you aim at. Believe it or not, even our police usually maintain only a minimum level of proficiency in this regard. The Los Angeles Police Department training statistics, for instance, show that in real-life gunfights, police officers miss their targets two out of three times at an average range of seven feet. That is not a misprint. Under the strain of combat you may not do any better.

Most people would do well to take a few lessons from someone who really knows what he is doing, such as a National Rifle Association certified instructor. Those who really want to master the firearm should look into one of the rifle, shotgun, or pistol courses offered by the American Pistol Institute (Box 401, Paulden, AZ 86336). There are some basic rules of thumb, however, which you can use to evaluate your ability with the gun.

Go to the range and set up a combat silhouette target seven to ten yards away. Fire three shots rapidly at the chest of the target with your pistol. These must be the first three shots of the day. If one of them misses, you need more practice.

For practice with a rifle, set the target about seventy-five yards away and conduct the same test. Remember, it is the first three shots of the day that count. No fair cheating by practicing for an hour and then testing yourself.

In practicing with a shotgun, set the target twenty-five to thirty yards away and fire one buckshot shell. You will want to see several holes in the torso of the target. If there are only one or two holes, the cause needs to be investigated. If it is a clean miss, you need a great deal more practice!

These are absolute minimum training standards of self-defense, and most shooting enthusiasts consider them very rudimentary. Even so, I hope that these guidelines assist you in your introduction to the world of firearms, which I have found interesting and somewhat enjoyable. Let me offer you one last piece of advice, though. In selecting your defensive firearms, never lose sight of the fact that the gun is a tool. It must be matched to both the shooter and the job at hand. Pistols are convenient when you are not expecting trouble, but when it appears at the door without warning. Rifles have greater penetration, range, and stopping power than pistols, and are vital if combat ranges exceed fifty yards, as they may in the street. Shotguns are devastating short-range weapons usually limited to a range of about forty yards maximum, such as around the house and in the yard. Pick weapons to fit your situation and your shooters for best results.

9. Your Home Is Your Castle. Stay There!

I used a broad base in writing this book because many of the preparations made for one disaster are the same as for another. However, they are not all alike, and specific information will help you weather your particular nightmare.

In researching this chapter, I found that in half the disasters the best action is to stay home, while in others the best idea is to leave the area immediately. In many cases you have no choice but to stay where you are. The disaster happens so fast that it catches you unaware. If you are at home, and have your supplies on hand, you can sit tight and wait until things get back to normal. Other disasters pose dangers that allow you no choice but to leave.

In this chapter I will discuss preparations for stay-at-home emergencies such as earthquakes, blizzards, blackouts, riots, and tornadoes. Run-for-your-life emergencies such as fires, hurricanes, chemical spills, floods, and nuclear reactor accidents will be discussed in the following chapter.

I would like to acknowledge the assistance of Gene Fear of the Survival Education Association (9035 Golden Given Road, Tacoma, WA 98445) who sent a variety of publications on surviving life's emergencies to me. The association produces an excellent selection of texts and visual aids for survival classes.

Earthquakes

Although California is known for its many earthquakes and faults (geological faults, that is), other states have their share, too. The biggest earthquake recorded in America was in Missouri in the 1800s. The central Rocky Mountain states are as dangerously unstable as California is, and in July 1980 an earthquake rated 5.1 on the Richter scale hit Kentucky and was felt in fourteen states from Michigan to Alabama. So it pays to be on your guard about earthquakes no matter where you live. If you live in southern California, it's that much more prudent to be ready for an earthquake. The U.S. Geological Society has predicted a serious earthquake in California sometime in the next few years.

The three main problems associated with earthquakes are:

1. Danger of falling debris injuring you.
2. Danger of fires starting from broken gas mains and fallen power lines.
3. The lack of emergency services for several days.

Emergency services are usually cut off by earthquakes because violent quakes drop bridges, topple telephone poles across roads, and worst of all, crumple fire station roofs on top of the trucks and ambulances as they did during the 1971 earthquake in Los Angeles. Then there are the overwhelming number of disaster victims demanding attention from agency personnel.

What should you do to protect yourself from falling debris? Find some place where falling glass and plasterboard—or even the roof—won't hit you. Crawl under a strong desk, table, workbench, or bed. Jumping inside your car isn't a bad idea if you happen to be in the garage when the quake strikes. The traditional advice of standing in a doorway during an earthquake is all right, but make sure it is a strong interior doorway away from windows, mirrors, and glass.

Despite your natural inclination, *don't* run outside. We always think of the outdoors as being safe, but have you ever noticed how many trees, power lines, and large buildings are near your home? You want to be someplace where things won't fall on you, and getting trapped under a falling balcony is not good survival strategy.

If there is great danger of more damage to your home or area from aftershocks, go to your backyard if it has no overhead dangers or to a large park or field you have checked out ahead of time, and wait for the aftershocks to pass. Sometimes they are more powerful than the original quake. Return to your home only when you are reasonably sure that the danger has passed.

You should have your stored food, water, and camping equipment in some accessible place. If your house has been damaged too severely to live in, it is wise to camp in your yard until you can find a permanent place to live. You can then protect your home from looters, put out small fires which might start, and be a lot more comfortable than you would be if you were crammed into a relief shelter with several hundred other people. Of course, if you can afford to stay in a hotel for two or three weeks, you may not view camping out as an attractive alternative, but most people can't plan on having that much money available on such short notice.

[URBAN ALERT!]

If your garage is still intact after the initial earthquake, immediately move your car out and park it in the street so an aftershock doesn't bury it under wreckage from the garage. Turn off the electricity and gas lines even if your house is unharmed to help prevent fires from broken lines in the event of strong aftershocks.

There are a lot of little things you can do to minimize earthquake damage to your home, too. My in-laws in Los Angeles cleverly installed childproof latches on all their cupboards, so that in the event of an earthquake, the cupboards will not fly open and spill their contents. This can save a tremendous amount of damage and cleanup afterwards, plus minimize the hazard of flying crockery. The American Red Cross recommends that you place large or heavy objects on lower shelves, and fasten shelves securely to walls. Also brace top-heavy objects. You should provide strong support for your water heater and other gas appliances to avoid fires starting from broken lines.

Blizzards

The main problem with many of these disasters is that they do not happen one at a time. Earthquakes and fires go together, hurricanes and floods are often co-events, and blizzards are frequently accompanied by blackouts and frozen water pipes. A good example of this was the cold spell in Boston, Massachusetts, reported in the *New York Times* on 11 January 1981. Although temperatures were only five to fifteen degrees below normal for that time of year, people and facilities were not prepared to handle even that slight temperature variation.

Just as there was a dangerously high demand for electricity due to the need for more home heating, the cold made the power lines brittle and more prone to snapping. There were hundreds of fires and scores of fatalities as people tried inventive ways to keep from freezing. It was so cold that the heating units in Boston Hospital could not keep up with the demand and personnel had to distribute extra blankets to keep the patients warm.

How would you fare in a blizzard? In a severe storm people are stuck where they are, hopefully at home. You You should be alert for warnings as the weather gets increasingly worse so you can get home and stay there. If the power goes out, you have your lamps and cookstove (remember to maintain adequate ventilation); if the water main bursts, you have your stored water and portable toilet; and if you can't walk to the store, you have enough food to feed your family. And if you live in cold country, you have a wood stove, if you are lucky, or a portable heater, or at least adequate clothes and blankets to keep you from freezing.

You should probably close off most of the house and live in one or two rooms, as your body heat will help keep the rooms warm and heating will take less of your fuel. Select a small room on the south side of the house, preferably not a corner room. Tape a layer of clear plastic film over the inside of the windows to limit heat loss, and take maximum advantage of incoming sunlight for warmth. Be sure to bring your portable toilet, bottled water, and food into the warmed room to keep them from freezing.

Keep your head and hands covered! Both head and hands are notorious radiators of body heat. At night, instead of leaving the heater on, family members should all bundle up together under blankets and turn off the heater and lights. In the morning you can heat the room up again, although it's awful being the first

Weather researchers predict that 7,000 tornadoes will hit the United States during the 1980s. A weather alert radio and a well-prepared hiding place in the house will minimize danger. See pages 106 and 107 for specific information.

one up! Make sure to dress warmly; thermal underwear makes all the difference in the world.

Drink plenty of warm fluids and don't go out of the house if it's difficult to see through the driving snow. Many people have perished within a few feet of their houses because they became disoriented and couldn't find their way back. Everything looks very different under several feet of snow, especially when a howling wind is blowing snowflakes into your eyes like sand. Don't forget to store a shovel in the house, too, in case you have to dig your way out when it's all over.

In the meantime, eat your stored food, and sit around playing games and telling stories. Make being snowbound an adventure rather than a life-threatening disaster. That's the difference being prepared makes.

Blackouts

Blackouts frequently accompany blizzards, but as we all know, they can happen at any time for a number of reasons. The worst problem with blackouts is that there is absolutely no warning before the lights go out. Because of this, it's very important to keep flashlights in strategic locations around the house, and to check the batteries every few months. A flashlight that doesn't work is worse than worthless; it's a broken promise. Make sure to keep extra batteries stored in your refrigerator for longer shelf life. We keep a flashlight beside our bed and one near the telephone in the exact center of the house, so that in an emergency, we are near at least one of them.

If the blackout lasts very long, you will find all the preparations suggested in this book to be invaluable. Adequate fuel, lanterns, cookers, food, and water will make even an extended blackout quite comfortable for you and your family. You will be very glad you don't have to go anywhere since, when the power is out, traffic lights don't function. Can you imagine driving across Los Angeles with no traffic lights?

No place is immune to blackouts, and they seem to happen a lot more often now than they used to. The increased power consumption has something to do with it, I suppose. In July 1981 high winds downed power lines in New Jersey and left sixty-seven thousand people there without electricity, and thousands more powerless in blackouts on Long Island and in Brooklyn, New York. The blackout in Nevada in February 1981 had an interesting twist though. About one-hundred-sixty-five thousand people were left without electricity overnight, but at the instant the power failed, some of the slot machines in the casinos went berserk and erupted coins. Now, that's the place to be in a power failure!

I do have one additional word of warning about blackouts. There is a consistent tendency to have a baby boom nine months after a blackout. This happened in New York after the blackouts and also after the Mount Saint Helen's eruption when everyone was required to stay inside in the dark for several days with nothing to do. Did you just think of something else to put in your emergency kit?

Riots

Riots are really scary because people act very unpredictably and do crazy and violent things they would never dream of doing under normal conditions. Riots are also frequently accompanied by blackouts, fires, and episodes of indiscriminate shooting and looting. This happened in the Miami, Florida, riot in July 1980 when thirty-three city blocks were without power, eighteen people lost their lives, seventy-nine or more rioters were arrested, and over one hundred million dollars in property damage was reported. I'm sure this was not the last riot this country will experience, and who knows where the next one will occur? It's good to be prepared.

If your neighborhood becomes a riot zone, keeping a low profile is a top priority. Stay at home and *stay away from the windows*. If there is shooting in front of your house, turn out the lights and go to the interior of your house. If you stand at the window and watch the action, one of two things is likely to happen. A rioter may shoot you just for fun, or the police might decide that you are a sniper and come in and arrest you. This happened in the Isla Vista, California, riots in 1969 when many innocent people were arrested only because they couldn't resist watching what was going on. The police are in a pretty untenable position during a riot and they get very jumpy. One police spokesman at the recent Miami, riots had this to say: "The police grabbed anything that was moving, so the situation was contained." Don't you be the "thing" that is moving when the police are trying to quell a riot.

Lock your doors and keep your shotgun handy in case someone tries to break in or set fire to your house. Use your stockpiled food so you won't have to go outside. Then wait for things to calm down. Do not, repeat, *do not* take your gun into the street unless you have a *very* good reason. In riots the police, and especially the ill-trained National Guardsmen, tend to look at the conflict as one between "us" and "them." If you are on the street with a gun, you are one of "them," and are likely to be shot on sight. There's plenty of time to ask questions at the coroner's inquest.

The only situation that might warrant your leaving home during a riot is fire. Better to make your way out of

Riots are frightening events because police, National Guardsmen, and rioters all act unpredictably due to strain. Unless fire threatens your home, making evacuation imperative, stay inside and away from windows.

the area than to be trapped in the middle of a raging fire. But think carefully about it first. It's dangerous out there, and if you are likely to survive where you are, it's probably better to keep your head down.

Tornadoes

Tornadoes are violently rotating columns of air which strike with frightening frequency over large parts of this country. Wind speeds reach two hundred miles an hour. In June 1980 twenty-four tornadoes were sighted by the National Weather Service in a two-day period. There were seven tornadoes in Indiana, four in Ohio, three in both Illinois and Texas, one in West Virginia, and two each in Michigan, Kentucky, and Pennsylvania. And this was only one flurry.

In fact, the National Oceanic and Atmospheric Administration predicts that the United States can expect at least 7,000 tornadoes during the 1980s, and that about 1,000 people will lose their lives in them. This prediction was based on the fact that there were 8,573 tornadoes during the 1970s and 986 people were killed. These are sobering statistics indeed.

Tornadoes are difficult because they happen so quickly and are so capricious. They will level a block of buildings, but leave one intact right in the middle of the devastation. If you live in a tornado-prone area, buy a weather alert radio. You can get one from Radio Shack (among other places) for about $40 (1980). Keep the radio plugged in all the time and it will alert you if a tornado watch has been issued by the weather service. The purpose of the watch is to give residents time to prepare before a tornado is actually sighted. If a watch is issued, ready your hiding place in the basement by clearing it of any small portable objects which can become deadly missiles in two-hundred-mile-an-hour winds. Tornadoes have been known to drive pieces of straw end-on into telephone poles like nails.

Make sure you prepare to take refuge against the wall closest to the expected approach of the tornado. If you don't have a basement, go to the lowest floor of the house to a windowless interior room, such as a closet, pantry, or bathroom. Collect blankets, coats, and pillows to build yourself a cocoon. Keep your portable radio tuned so you will know immediately when a tornado watch becomes a *tornado warning*. A warning means that a tornado has been sighted and you and your radio should take cover until the danger is over.

Afterward, all you have to do is pick up the pieces. You will probably have lost no more than a few shingles and a tree limb here and there, but if your neighborhood has been badly hit, you will need your survival supplies and some heavy tools. Crowbars, axes, saws, and shovels are essential for digging yourself out of the wreckage of your house, if there is any, removing your supplies and belongings from the wreckage, and rescuing your neighbors who may be trapped in the splinters of their homes. Store these tools in your tornado shelter so they will be there when you need them.

10. Run for Your Life

Although this book is intended mainly for people who live in cities and who are reluctant to leave home even in the face of a major disaster, there are some situations where a prudent person packs up and drives away. You don't want to be home if there is a fire, hurricane, flood (especially a flash flood), chemical spill, or nuclear reactor accident threatening you. Preparations for an emergency evacuation involve special, lightweight compact automobile survival kits which are discussed in detail in chapter 13.

Fire

Fires happen literally *all* the time. When I was researching this book I looked up fires in the *New York Times Index* and found pages of references to articles about serious fires. I was astounded. One article about the National Fire Data Center said that most fires are caused by improper use of heating equipment and that the southeast United States has the highest death rate due to fire in the world. Fatalities in individual states there range from forty-six to seventy-eight per million. Only Alaska has a higher rate with eighty-eight deaths per million. Alaskans use their heaters nearly all year and have more opportunities for accidents.

[URBAN ALERT!]

Because fires are so common, there are a number of measures you need to take to protect yourself and your family. Firstly, you should install a smoke detector in your home. Secondly, you should buy a couple of large fire extinguishers. With these you might be able to put out a small fire before it becomes a big fire. Thirdly, you and your family should learn several exits out of your house, even if it means climbing through windows. You have to be able to reach these exits while crawling along the floor in the dark.

Plan for the entire family to meet at some location out of the house. Many lives have been tragically lost by parents going into burning buildings after missing children when the children were actually safe, but not in sight. Don't let this happen to you. With a planned rendezvous, you can quickly find out if someone is missing while there is still time to save him or her.

You should post the emergency phone number for the fire department on your phone for quick reference. And most importantly, you should drill your entire family periodically so each member knows what to do. After losing her home in the Santa Barbara, California, fire in 1977, my sister started having fire drills for her two daughters ages three and eleven. She found that the first thing they did when she yelled "fire" was to run looking for her. After several tries, they became confident that they knew what to do and, rather than looking for their mother, quickly went to the safe rendezvous outside. Make sure your children know what to do before their lives depend on it.

But what should you do if the fire is a few blocks away and heading toward you? The first thing is to resist the temptation to go and watch the firemen. The fire department does not need spectators, and sightseeing draws your attention away from the danger your house

[110]

may be in. If there is a fire in your area, pack up and *prepare to leave.* Then do your sightseeing from a safe distance.

Now let me tell you the story of what happened to my sister as there are many lessons to be learned from her experience. At first the fire was quite far away and she and her neighbors were outside watching it, when it suddenly jumped a back road and advanced toward their homes from behind. When she and her husband realized what was happening, they ran around the house gathering all their prized possessions and putting them into the car. My sister put the car keys on the bed so she would know where they were. Her husband used the bedspread to collect things and carry them to the car. By this time, it was getting dark and the fire had burned down the power lines.

When the flames burned so close that my sister and her husband had to flee, they couldn't find the misplaced car keys in the dark. They had no flashlight. If it hadn't been for a friend who stopped by to pick them up, they might not have gotten away alive from the fire. As it was, they had only five minutes to spare, and they lost all their valuables when the house and the hastily packed car both burned.

People naturally tend to panic when threatened by a fire, so it's tremendously helpful if you prepare beforehand so you don't have to depend on thinking clearly in a crisis. A good example of the psychological stresses involved is the story of my brother-in-law and his jewelry box. He had a favorite ring that he wanted to save from the fire. He opened the small jewelry box, took the ring, and left the box. The box could easily have fit into his pocket and he would have saved *all* his jewelry from the fire, but he was just not thinking straight. Panic does that.

[URBAN ALERT!]

The best way to save all those family treasures you would hate to lose in a fire is to make a list of the items and their locations and keep it in a special place along with a spare set of car keys, a flashlight, and a duffel bag. At the last minute, you can rush through the house collecting your valuables and tossing them in the bag just before you drive away. This technique is described in detail in chapter 13.

There is a more mundane side to the devastation caused by a fire. The paperwork involved in making a list of everything you lose when your house burns is staggering, so keeping an up-to-date inventory of your valuables will make your life much easier if you ever have to file an insurance claim. We have taken pictures of every room of our house with all the drawers and closets open. It looks like a real mess, but the photographs will be invaluable if the house ever burns. This method is a lot faster and easier than making a detailed inventory list, but the list is better because it contains important information on dates of purchase, serial numbers, and costs of replacement which the photos don't provide. We sent a duplicate set of the photos and inventory to relatives for safekeeping. It wouldn't do to have the pictures burn along with the house!

Keep all your business papers with your inventory so you can pick them up quickly. When you are reestablishing your life, it's advantageous to have with you the registration slips for your cars, your insurance papers, and all those other vital documents you need to manage your complex life.

Be sure to keep your insurance coverage at replacement cost values. With the way inflation is going, having your home insured for fifty thousand dollars when it will cost you one hundred thousand dollars to rebuild will leave you in deep financial trouble. After a fire, you have enough trauma to handle, so don't invite financial worries.

I know this all seems like a lot of work, and it is. But don't put off preparing until it's too late. Why not set aside one hour each week to work on your preparations until they are complete? You'll find that you'll make a lot of progress in that first hour, and you'll sleep easier afterward.

Here is another scenario to prepare for in advance. You are at home and a fire starts nearby. The kids are at school and your spouse is at work. The phones go out, so you can't call anyone. You have drilled and know what to do, so you pack the car and get out. Meanwhile, the family finds out about the fire and begins to worry. Arrange ahead of time for someplace to go. Preplanning will prevent your spouse from going to the burning area to look for you. Go to your rendezvous and call your family immediately to tell them you are safe. This is imperative. How would you feel if you thought any of your family might be in the fire? You know you are safe; you should arrange a method to let them know, too. Each member of the family who is old enough to be home alone should be drilled on all phases of leaving the home, then letting the others know he or she is safe.

Floods

Floods are common springtime occurrences, many times in totally unexpected places. An example of this was the flood in Phoenix, Arizona, in February 1980 when eleven thousand residents were evacuated and half of the population of the city was trapped at home by high waters. This flood was of a scope seen only once in five hundred years, and this time it was Arizona's turn. Eight of the ten bridges over the Salt River that runs through Phoenix were closed, which indicates why it's

Floods are common occurrences in the spring and when a new dam is being filled. Usually the National Weather Service gives warning in time to evacuate. Getting out when you are told will save you being caught in a scene like this one.

so important to locate several ways out of your area. Half the city's one and a half million people were isolated, and twelve hundred residents lost their power due to trees falling across telephone and power lines.

The best way to avoid the trauma of watching your house float away is to check out the area before you buy or rent. Many houses are being built in the middle of flood plains, and the people who buy them are asking for trouble. Maybe it will take ten or twenty years, but eventually they will be flooded out. Check with your local civil defense personnel before investing your money into certain heartbreak. They usually maintain maps showing which areas are in danger from floods for use in an emergency.

Dams can pose the other real flooding danger to your home. The Army Corps of Engineers is supposed to check all dams for safety, but they just don't seem to get around to it. The most dangerous time for flooding is when a new dam is filling for the first time, as it was in the case of the Teton Dam disaster. If there is a new dam upstream of your area, make a habit of spending stormy nights in motels on high ground. If there happens to be an unplanned dam in your area, be especially cautious. Some incredible disasters have happened in Pennsylvania when dams of slag have washed out.

But if you already live in a potential flood zone and can't or don't want to move, what are you supposed to do? The factor that makes floods easier to survive than some other disasters is that at least you have a little warning. In many areas, the worst flood threat is spring runoff, and you can spend weeks preparing for it. Get a weather alert radio and keep it plugged in. Then if the waters start to pose a threat, the radio will turn itself on and alert you. When it does, don't equivocate. Load your car with your last-minute items and go to high ground.

Check for several routes out of the area. While driving over these potential escape routes, look carefully for places where the water on the road may be unexpectedly deep. If the water on the street is six to eight inches deep, you can probably drive through. But if there is a spot along the way where the road crosses a minor depression, the water during a storm might be deep enough to stall your car and leave you stranded.

We have to contend with high water whenever we visit relatives in Orange County, California, during the winter rainy season. Heavy rains flood the streets there, and over the years we have had to learn a roundabout route through back streets and parking lots to avoid the deep drainage gutters county officials seem to prefer to underground storm drains. We once had the wake of another car break over the front of our hood like a wave while we were crossing one of those idiotic deepwater intersections. If your life depends on your driving through flooded streets, you'd better know the terrain. Remember, it's not the average water depth, but the deepest spot, that concerns you. Find the roads with the highest and most level surfaces to make your exit.

The most important thing to remember when you are trying to decide whether or not it's time to abandon your house is that your life is more important than your home. Be on the safe side, and leave before you have to risk your life to do so. Remember, too, that the water will continue to rise even after the rain stops. So wait a while before deciding that the danger has passed.

Hurricanes

Hurricanes are storms that originate over tropical oceans and have winds of at least 74 miles per hour. They are very violent storms and are nothing to fool around with. A good example of the destructive poten-

tial of a hurricane came in August 1980 with Hurricane
Allen. It killed 102 people and winds in Haiti were
recorded at 185 miles per hour. News reports say that
260,000 people were evacuated in Texas and Mexico and
that there were millions of dollars of damage. In
Brownsville, Texas, the hurricane winds were accompanied by tornadoes, floods, power failures, and a failure of the city water system. How's that for a lot of
trouble all at once?

During hurricanes, as with tornadoes and floods,
your best friend is your weather alert radio. It will turn
itself on and let you know when there is danger in
enough time for you to get out. Have your gear packed
and ready and in the car. Civil defense authorities have
experience in evacuating people who are in the path of
hurricanes, so when they say you should leave, don't
argue. Do it. I still don't recommend going to official
refugee centers, though, especially if you are prepared.
The officials are quite likely to confiscate everything
you brought, food, medicine, equipment, and all. It's
better to just drive out of the area for a few days of rainy
vacation. Head northwest and visit the Great Plains.

Chemical Spills and Train Wrecks

I am including train derailments with chemical spills
because much of the chemical hazard we experience
today is the result of wrecked tank cars releasing poisonous or explosive gases. Train wrecks happen so
often that they aren't usually considered interesting
news. But trains transport almost all the extremely
hazardous material moved throughout the nation.

Two factors add to the dangers posed by wrecked tank
cars carrying chemicals. Firstly, a tank car is a very
large container that when ruptured can release many
tons of chemicals. Secondly, emergency service person-

nel frequently don't know what is in the cars, and don't understand the potential hazards once the contents are known. We knew a civil defense director who discovered in the nick of time that a burning boxcar was carrying radioactive wastes. Some of these wastes explode if water is sprayed on them.

I once worked for a university chemistry department, and was surprised at how often the fire department called our professors to ask about the hazards of chemicals that had spilled on the nearby tracks. I was very unsettled when I realized that it takes the clean-up crews at least an hour to find out what kind of hazards they are dealing with, and much longer than that for them to get around to evacuating the people who might be affected. Be alert and take action yourself when there has been a train wreck in your neighborhood.

We have been very fortunate to not have a major train derailment disaster in the last few years, although there are twenty or thirty near-misses each year in which people are hastily evacuated from the area around ruptured or burning tank cars. In August 1981 a train's brakes failed in San Luis Potosi, Mexico, and a smashed chlorine gas car killed at least eight people and forced the evacuation of over eight hundred more. In July 1980 four thousand people in Kentucky were evacuated when a train carrying six carloads of explosive vinyl chloride and one of liquid chlorine gas caught on fire. The resulting poisonous fumes would have covered Louisville, except that the wind shifted at the last minute. As it was, the four thousand evacuees were not allowed to return to their homes for four days. Incidents like this one can happen any place there's a railroad track.

But train derailments are not the only kind of chemical spills that happen. The other vulnerable sites are oil

Fire, frightening in itself, is doubly so when it involves a
chemical spill or plant explosion. This photo was taken at an
oil refinery fire in Whiting, Indiana, in 1955.

refineries and chemical manufacturing plants. In May 1980 at Woods Cross, Utah, a Phillips Petroleum plant experienced three successive explosions in which flames shot two hundred feet in the air. This is an oil plant which processes twenty-five thousand barrels of oil a day. Fortunately, the fires were contained with only eight people hospitalized and a nearby trailer court evacuated. But it could have been much worse.

Let this be a warning to you if you live near a plant of this type. When you hear an explosion, see a fire, or see a funny green cloud coming near, don't take time to investigate. Just *leave* for a while. Let your radio tell you how bad the disaster was. Don't become one of the statistics.

One of the scariest incidents of problems in chemical manufacturing occurred in Sevaso, Italy, in 1976. The plant had an accident, and one of the unknown by-products of the accident was a small amount of a deadly poison called dioxin. It took several weeks of continuing and extensive complaints from the residents whose farm animals were dying all around them before the officials looked into it. It turned out that the people were being poisoned too. Not only did they require medical attention, but they also had to be *permanently* evacuated from their homes because there is no known way of decontaminating the area. Even burning the building won't work because dioxin isn't detoxified by fire. Don't take chances when something funny is going on at the local chemical plant. Run for your life—to the upwind side of the plant, of course.

Nuclear Reactor Accidents

I added this section because of the prominence the Three Mile Island incident had in the news. If you live near a nuclear power plant, you probably have made up your mind either to move or to ignore the problem. The trouble is that there are more and more plants being built, leaving more and more people in the precarious position of having to trust the power companies to safely operate the plants.

The scariest thing about a nuclear reactor accident is something that was vividly demonstrated at Three Mile Island. The authorities outside the plant did not know what had happened and the power company people were quite slow about informing the public that there was even a slight problem. In fact, it was three days before they admitted the full extent of the accident. Learn from this, and if there is any hint of a problem at your local nuclear plant, *leave the area.* You can always come back later if it turns out to be a false alarm, but in the meantime, your life is not in jeopardy. Though the media made very little mention of this fact, over 40 percent of the residents of the surrounding area spontaneously left town during the emergency. They had their priorities straight. The remaining people must have had a great deal of faith in the safety of the plant.

If you live near a nuclear plant, you need a low-range radiation detection alarm. It goes off like a smoke alarm if an unusual amount of radiation suddenly enters the atmosphere. These devices are very expensive at about a thousand dollars apiece, but you should consider them part of the cost of living near a reactor.

There must be hundreds of books written on the subject of nuclear reactor plants, and they are almost all severely biased either for or against them. Two books I recommend are *We Almost Lost Detroit* by John G. Fuller and *The Health Hazards of NOT Going Nuclear* by Petr Beckmann. The first book takes an antinuclear stand and will give you a deep appreciation of the hazards and problems of nuclear technology. The second book is pronuclear and will assure you that Fuller does not know what he is talking about.

Take your pick. Personally, I wouldn't want to be standing at the fence waiting for the official bulletins during the next "malfunction."

11. We Won't Glow in the Dark

If nuclear war is your concern, you are not alone. With the situation in the Middle East as it is and the Soviet invasion of Afghanistan, Americans have finally begun to realize the precariousness of our global situation. So what happens if the bombs are dropped? We are all vaporized, right? Wrong. My husband has written the book *Life After Doomsday,* (Paladin Press, P.O. Box 1307, Boulder, CO 80306) which goes into nuclear war survival preparations in great depth. If you are really interested in nuclear war, get his book. But if you are only a little worried about nuclear war and don't want to go to the trouble of making first-class preparations, here is a quickie course on what equipment you need to get to survive a nuclear war and how to use it.

First, in talking about nuclear war, we have to dispel some of the many myths about it. We will not all be vaporized, for instance. Hoping for the first bomb to fall on you will do no good. Over half of the American population will still be alive and uninjured after a full-scale nuclear attack on the United States. So what if the "lucky" ones were killed instantly? What about you? You will have your food, water, and the other supplies discussed in previous chapters of this book, so you will be a long step ahead of the other survivors. Now let me tell you what you need to know to keep from losing your lead—and maybe your life.

Who is going to be attacked with these nuclear weapons? All the people who live in big cities like you do, right? Wrong again. The cities are not targets just because lots of people are there. You got that idea from our government's policy of mutual assured destruction, but the Soviet Union never agreed to it. They are interested in military targets only. When your goal is world conquest, you don't waste expensive missiles on tract houses.

Some cities include targets; others don't. And even if there is a target within Los Angeles or New York, where there are several, just because the target gets a bomb does not mean that you will have ended all your worries. Quite the contrary. The danger zone of a one-megaton bomb (the most common kind in the Soviet arsenal) extends only thirteen miles from the target. If you are farther than that from the target, you're going to be a very excited spectator, not a casualty. The warheads these days are so accurate that we don't have to worry much about them missing their targets. So if you live more than thirteen miles from a target, you can just about figure on surviving the attack unless you are the victim of an accident.

So what are the targets? First, and most obvious are the military installations which are our missile, bomber, and submarine bases. Then come commercial airports big enough for jets to land. The jets, too, are valuable targets. After that are the electrical power plants, including nuclear and hydroelectric ones. The philosophy behind these three priorities is as follows:

1. Military bases are hit so they can't shoot back.

2. Airports are hit so we can't transfer troops for them or use them as alternate bomber bases.

3. Power plants are hit to devastate the morale of the American public and to hinder the resumption of our industrial output, communications, and normal lifestyle.

After these three major types of targets come the more traditional, lower-priority targets. All major heavy industries will be in danger, such as coal mining, steel milling, and auto manufacturing. Seaports will be bombed as will large railroad yards to slow industrial recovery and deployment of troops. That about covers the targets, and it's enough to depress anyone anyway. But don't forget the punchline: You *can* survive nuclear war. It's not that difficult to overcome the problems, even the problem of fallout.

What about fallout anyway? Most people don't know that fallout is just radioactive dirt. It sifts down out of the mushroomlike cloud during the first day after the attack. Since the cloud can blow hundreds of miles in a day, fallout can rain down over large areas many miles downwind from the target. Another fact most people don't know is that fallout happens only after ground bursts like those used to smash missile silos. Cities and airfields are damaged more efficiently by air bursts which produce large blast areas, but do not cause fallout.

Let me explain what you are up against in surviving nuclear fallout. The three kinds of fallout radiation are alpha, beta, and gamma. Alpha rays are inconsequential compared to beta and gamma rays because even a single sheet of paper will stop alpha particles cold. Beta and gamma rays are more penetrating, so if you are protected from them, you will also be protected from the alpha particles.

Beta rays can be stopped by as little as five inches of air between you and the fallout grains. Beta radiation becomes dangerous if you get fallout grains on your skin. Then you develop raw sores called beta burns which are quite ugly, but which will eventually heal like a badly skinned knee. They are something you would like to avoid, however, especially since they may become infected if they are not kept clean.

The life-threatening problem in a fallout emergency is the gamma radiation. You need heavy mass protection to the tune of at least 150 pounds per square foot of wall to stop gamma rays. That's why you need a fallout shelter, preferably, underground where it is easy to surround yourself with massive walls. That's the bad news about gamma rays. The good news is the rapid rate of deterioration of the radiation. Let me first tell you the numbers you need to know. Later I will tell you about the shelters you need to build in order to achieve a low radiation dose.

Gamma radiation is the hazard which can quickly kill you in a fallout emergency. It is measured in *rads* and the rate of exposure is called *rads/hr*. The chart below lists results of total dosages. The results of each dose are based on the assumption that all the radiation was received within a few days. If this much radiation was received over a month or a year, the effects would be much less severe.

Total Rads Received

25 — No noticeable effect in adults other than slight increases in the cancer rate many years later.

100 — A few people will develop radiation sickness (nausea) but all will recover. Two persons in 1,000 will eventually get leukemia who would not ordinarily have gotten it.

200 — Most people will exhibit the symptoms of radiation sickness such as vomiting and increased susceptibility to infections; 1 in 100 will die of radiation sickness. This figure assumes that full medical care is available. Mortality rates will be substantially higher in an actual attack.

450 — Fifty out of 100 people will die of radiation sickness even with the best medical care, so most people sustaining this amount of radiation will die after an actual attack.

There are two kinds of radiation meters you need so you can keep track of your radiation dosage. The first is a high-range gamma survey meter. The cheapest way to get one is to make one. Both my husband's book, *Life After Doomsday,* and Cresson Kearny's book, *Nuclear War Survival Skills* (each available for $8.95 in paperback from Survival, Inc.) contain templates and specific instructions on how to build the Kearny Fallout Meter using common household materials. It can be put together in a matter of hours from items usually found in the kitchen. But be forewarned; don't try to copy the directions for a friend. The templates in the plans are distorted by xeroxing, so copies make faulty meters. Just what you need, right?

If you don't want to go to the trouble of making your own meter, you can buy a high-range survey meter from Victoreen (10101 Woodland Avenue, Cleveland, OH 44104). If you are interested, ask about the current availability of high-range gamma meters. Our experience has been that the model numbers and prices change faster than we can keep up with in print.

You need a meter which measures gamma radiation rates of exposure in the range of roughly 0-500 rads/hr,

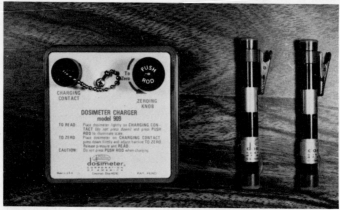

Self-calibrating high-range radiation meters like this one from Nuclear Emergency Services (*top*) are essential for nuclear war survival preparation. Pen-sized dosimeters (*bottom*) keep track of a person's radiation dosage when worn at belt-height. Each member of the family needs one.

which is a very high range. This type of meter is important because most of those you normally come across in medical and scientific laboratories measure only in the range of 0-0.1 rads/hr. This will do you no good if you need to know how much fallout radiation is present. Some of the low-range meters give inaccurately low readings when overloaded, so it's very dangerous to depend on them in an attack.

When you are using a high-range meter to measure fallout, be sure to hold it exactly three feet above the ground. The radiation is more intense near the fallout particles on the ground, and drops off with height. The exposure tables assume that the measurements are made at three feet.

The second meter you need is a personal dosimeter which measures total accumulated dosage for one person. The meter lets you know exactly how much exposure an individual has had, so every member of your family should have one. One dosimeter charger will do for the entire family. A model 686 dosimeter which measures 0-600 rads is available from Victoreen for about $82 (1981). Again, this is an unusually high range. So do not get the common 100 millirad (0.1 rad) dosimeter used in laboratories. Wear this pencil-sized piece of equipment on your belt to measure an average body dose. The lower half of your body is closer to the fallout on the ground, so if you wear the dosimeter at your collar level, its accuracy will be considerably off.

Now you know what you are up against. So you are sitting in your shelter and the fallout is coming down. How long do you have to stay there? Here is the 7:10 rule to help you calculate. After seven times as much time, there will be only one-tenth the radiation. For example, seven hours after the explosion, there will be only one-tenth as much radiation as at one hour after the explosion. At forty-nine hours (7 x 7), there will be one-hundredth (10 x 10) as much, and at slightly more than two weeks (49 x 7), there will be one-thousandth (100 x 10) as much radiation. Sounds much better, doesn't it? This is why civil defense shelters always used to be stocked for only two weeks. See? You can survive nuclear war, fallout, and radiation. It's not so hard.

You know you want to keep your radiation exposure as low as possible, and definitely below the 200-rad threshold of lethal exposure. You also know that the radiation will diminish rapidly. When can you go out? When the radiation level according to your gamma meter is down to 2 rads/hr, you can go out for a total of three hours per day, if you have to. This is not to say you should take a Sunday stroll to see how the neighborhood has fared. But it might be smart to go out and decontaminate your house and surrounding area to reduce the amount of residual radiation you are receiving.

Hose down the roof and pavement surrounding your residence, and if you have a long-handled push broom, scrub the crevices to help further. Wash the fallout away from the house into a trench, hole, or drain, or over the edge of the curb into the gutter. Exposing yourself briefly during this decontamination effort will give both you and your family less radiation exposure in the long run. But check constantly to be sure that you are not getting more than 2 rads/hr in the process.

If you are going out to decontaminate your house, or to put out a fire while the fallout is still falling, which is very risky business, but better than burning, take some precautions. Wear a rainsuit of sorts. Expensive radiation suits are sold to keep the beta radiation away from your skin, but any good covering will do. Remember to completely cover yourself, especially your head and hair. It's also a good idea to have a dust mask to filter out particles and keep them from lodging in your lungs.

Whether or not you have a radiation suit, you must thoroughly decontaminate yourself when you come back inside. Take a shower and pay particular attention to cleaning your hair and the folds of your skin. These are the places where the fallout particles are most likely to lodge. Don't forget your eyelids and behind your ears. Be thorough.

If you begin to itch, the beginning symptoms of beta burns, wash the area again thoroughly. A burn might still develop, but at least you will have removed the particles. Beta burns should be treated much like skinned knees, keep them clean and they will eventually heal. If they don't get infected, they won't even scar. Remember that radiation sickness makes infections more likely and harder to cure.

You were worried about nuclear war; you found out you could, and probably would survive; you bought your radiation meters, and now you need a fallout shelter. I will again recommend *Life After Doomsday,* which contains a full-length discussion of most types of fallout shelters you can buy or build yourself. *Nuclear War Survival Skills* discusses six shelters, three of which are above-ground shelters for use in areas with high water tables. These shelters have been thoroughly tested and built by people who are not carpenters under the supervision of Oak Ridge National Laboratory researchers in less than forty-eight hours using materials readily available in most homes. This is probably the best way to go if you don't want to construct a permanent fallout shelter.

A word of warning, though. The Federal Emergency Management Agency (FEMA) has a nifty little book called *In Time of Emergency* which they are ready to

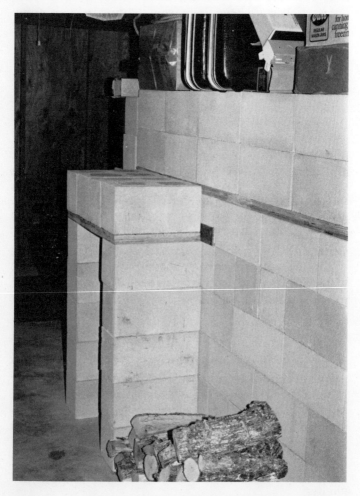

Our portable fallout shelter (*top*), built in the garage, has walls two feet thick and weighs several tons, but when we move, we'll dismantle it. Most Americans will initially survive a nuclear bomb blast (*right*). Preparations will keep fallout and radiation sickness from slowly killing them.

distribute in a time of crisis. Although this book has plans for expedient shelters, some of these plans haven't been changed since the early 1950s. Apparently they haven't been tested by FEMA either because some of the shelters cave in on their occupants. Others have such poor ventilation that they would cause suffocation. The government strikes again!

This is a good example of why you should go to the expense and trouble of making your own disaster preparations rather than simply trusting in the government to take care of you.

To suit our needs, we built a removable shelter in the garage. We wanted a temporary fallout shelter for a location where excavating would be very difficult, so we built a very austere shelter made of 490 concrete blocks with six tons of gravel in the cores for a total cost of $700 for materials. The walls are two feet thick with gravel filling the cores of the blocks. Bruce has calculated that its protection factor is about 40 which would protect us in most cases. This protection factor would cut down our radiation exposure by 97 percent and matches officially recommended protection levels. Later on, when we can make arrangements for a better shelter, we'll disassemble this one and put the car back in the garage.

But these shelters all take time to build and a strong sense of purpose. You would feel like a fool digging up your backyard or, worse yet, the vacant lot down the street, and having nothing happen. So you will probably tend to do nothing. Well, there's still hope. Anything is better than nothing. So when the civil defense alarms go off, and you realize this is it, here's what to do. Remember when I said you need 150 pounds per square foot of weight between you and the radiation? That's what you want to achieve. Now it doesn't matter what that weight consists of—books, water, or bricks will do equally well. So if you have a basement—lucky you—go to the deepest corner and put a couple of sturdy chests of drawers together to form the two ends of your shelter. Cover them with two or three interior doors from your closets or bedrooms to form a sturdy table. Remember, the bigger your shelter is, the more weight you are going to have to find to surround it, so make it small. Then pile everything heavy you can find on top of the doors and around the sides of the shelter. Leave a small doorway.

One neat trick is to fill your garbage cans and wastebaskets with water to form part of your walls. Water is really heavy, weighing eight pounds per gallon. Don't be afraid to use your stored water for the walls. The radiation won't hurt the water as long as it's covered from direct exposure to the fallout grains. Radiation passing through objects heats them very slightly, but it does not make them radioactive.

If your basement has a workbench, you can use it instead of the interior doors, as long as the workbench is sturdy. You will be cozy, even cramped, but your confinement won't last too long. Being in the corner of the basement, the surrounding earth will protect you on the two exterior sides. You have now built a makeshift monstrosity. If it isn't 150 pounds per square foot of wall, don't worry about it. It's better than what you had, which was nothing. It may save your life anyway.

If you don't have a basement, build the same shelter in the very center of your house, under the highest part of the roof. You are trying to keep as much distance and mass between you and the fallout as possible. If you live in an apartment building, you might be better off than being in a low-slung house. If it's a multifloor building, check first to see if there is a subbasement. That's the best place. Otherwise, find a central corridor or room on an intermediate floor. Try to be at least three floors up from the street and another three down from the roof. This way you will be best protected from the fallout on the roof, ground, and exterior walls.

We are almost done. The only thing left is ventilation. In the small closed cubbyhole you have built for yourself and your family, the heat and carbon dioxide generated by your bodies can make life pretty uncomfortable, or even impossible. So you do need to arrange for ventilation. Kearny's book contains detailed instructions for constructing both a makeshift air pump which looks like a Venetian blind on a swinging frame, and a fan which circulates the air through the shelter using a large cardboard paddle. Don't be afraid to let unfiltered air into the shelter as long as it's not visibly carrying in dust with it. Fallout is not like poison gas. The poison gas you need to worry about is the carbon dioxide from your own breathing. Ventilation is vital.

12. The Three-Day Test

At several points in this book I have mentioned the Three-Day Test that I took and failed miserably. Let me explain at this point what it is and its purpose.

The Three-Day Test was designed by Bill Pier of Survival, Inc. to graphically demonstrate the shortcomings of most survival programs. It's the only valid way to comfortably judge your ability to survive short-term emergencies. It has a hidden advantage, too. While some of your family members might be reluctant to participate in the test, once they see the need for preparing, they will become willing participants in your preparations. At least that's what happened to me.

The rules of the test are as follows. First, turn off your water, electricity, and gas. You should already know where these shutoffs are located in case of an emergency. Now I realize that it may not be practical for you to turn them all off, especially if you live in an apartment building. But do make a point of finding out where they are. In an emergency, you may be the only one who knows.

If you can't turn off your services, make sure you don't use them. You can turn off the water using the shutoff valves under the sinks and behind the toilets. Unplug everything in your house. Turn off your thermostat. Put

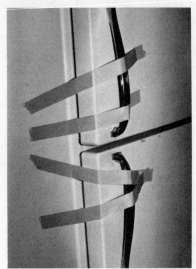

In the Three-Day Test, we taped the light switches, toilet, and refrigerator to make them inoperative and remind ourselves not to use them.

tape over all the light switches. The exceptions I made to the plan were the refrigerator and freezer. I did not unplug them, but neither did I use them. I taped the doors shut. Remember that in a real emergency, you will have all that thawing food to deal with, either by canning, smoking, or drying it, or throwing out what you can't eat. We have a quarter of beef in the freezer, and I hate to think about wasting it. Food will stay frozen for a couple of days in an unopened freezer, though, depending on how full the freezer is and how hot the weather is.

Some people cannot take three days away from work or school, but even if you go to work one of the three days, you must abide by some rules. You are not to eat or drink anything that you did not bring from home. You must use only the gasoline you have in your car at the time of the test, or what you had stored for emergencies ahead of time.

You have unplugged the TV and agreed not to make calls on the telephone, but what about the radio? You are allowed one-half hour per day listening to your battery-powered radio, since that amount would probably be available on a limited basis during an emergency. But don't read the newspapers or your mail, because part of the test includes the psychological stress of the isolation involved. All set? *Now do it.* The key to this test is to do it on the spur of the moment, not when you are ready for it.

The toughest part of the test is lasting for three days. The first twenty-four hours are the hardest; that's when our first test broke down. But try to stick it out, and if the flaws you find in your planning are so bad that you do quit, make sure you fill the gaps in your preparation, and try it again. It's only a true test if you last for the full three days. Good luck!

[THE THREE-DAY TEST]

Our First Try

Let me tell you what happened to me. It might make you feel better when you run into problems. My husband and I and our six-month-old son did our test in 1980 while living in Los Angeles, California. We had been interested in preparation for several years, and though we didn't have a lot of money to work with, we thought we would get along just fine. We had plenty of canned food, stored water, a backpacking stove and fuel, disposable diapers for the baby, kerosene lamps, and even a portable toilet. Living three days without utilities would pose no problems at all, we thought. But we barely lasted twenty-four hours and had some hair-raising experiences in even that short time.

We started our test one Friday morning before breakfast. My husband then went to work for the day, leaving me home with the baby and no facilities. The day proceeded with no real problems, but it lasted a long, long time. With no TV, radio, or stereo, I was getting pretty bored after eight hours of reading. My husband came home that evening saying, "This is easy."

We fixed our dinner on the backpacking stove, and settled in for the evening. That's when we learned our first lesson. We had a pair of kerosene wick lamps, and although they were good for atmosphere, they were poor to read by. But that wasn't the worst problem. When Bruce stumbled over the baby who was crawling around in the dark part of the living room, we realized that we definitely needed more lamps. And when we had to go into the bathroom to change the baby's pants, we discovered that it took two people to do the job: one to hold the lamp, and one to hold the baby. The lamp had a wide slippery bottom that was difficult to hold firmly in one hand, and Bruce says the same was true of the baby.

Immediately we realized that we needed at least one lamp that was easy to hold and carry with one hand.

But these were not insurmountable obstacles, and we were pleased to learn these things. Our next adjustment was the discovery that with the dim light and inactivity, eight o'clock seemed like midnight. There was nothing to do but go to bed. The next morning six o'clock and daylight were quite inviting. That was how quickly our schedules started to revolve around the sun instead of artificial light.

So we got up, but the water was turned off and not getting our morning showers was quite an adjustment. Then, as Bruce was boiling water for our breakfast, we had a little problem with the camp stove. It practically exploded. This was a little backpacking stove which overheated and started burning out of control. It was a roaring ball of flame on our kitchen counter. Fortunately, we had a fire extinguisher in the kitchen for just such an emergency, and we put the fire out within seconds. So much for our hot breakfast. But it didn't really discourage us once visions of the house burning down faded, because we had selected our canned food stockpile to be edible even without heat. We told each other that we could just have cold meals for a couple of days. No big deal.

And then came the straw that broke the camel's back. We owned a portable toilet which we used in our camper, but we thought that for the test we would save all our waste water from doing dishes and bathing and use it to flush the toilet once a day. We thought that this method would conserve water and still let us use the toilet. There were only two problems with this theory.

The first was the smell. We were two adults with a baby in diapers. Neglecting to flush the toilet for twenty-four hours produced an odor which wilted the plastic roses on the back of the toilet. Anything else would have been better.

The second problem was that after twenty-four hours of conserving water, there still was not enough gray water to flush our toilet. We had carefully used only a minimum amount of wash and rinse water while doing dishes, and had recycled the rinse water as wash water for the next meal. We had saved all our bathing and toothbrushing water, too, but the total amount came to less than three gallons by the morning of the second day. We had to pour an additional two gallons of fresh water into the toilet to get it to flush. We later learned that pouring the water directly into the bowl to flush it, rather than into the back of the toilet, takes less water.

Although we had stored plenty of water for the Three-Day Test, we wanted to find out how much we needed for future reference. Extravagant use of our water would not have given us the information we needed and wasting half of our water on toilet flushing wasn't a good idea.

But all was not lost; we were still prepared. We had the portable toilet. All we had to do was get it out of the garage, and carry on. Or did we? Just when we needed it most, we found out that the metal rod which operated the valve between the bowl and the holding tank had corroded in place, making the toilet utterly useless.

So there we were, two survivalists—eating cold food (at least our hand-powered can opener still worked), and looking forward to a long, dark night in a house that smelled less than lovely. At least we had enough water. We then decided to call off the test, better prepare ourselves, and try again.

We learned all of this marvelous information in a mere twenty-four hours. It was humiliating but what we learned might one day make real survival a lot more bearable. How will you fare in your test?

Our Successful Test

We learned a lot on our first try, but could not be sure we were prepared for a real interruption of services until we had successfully completed three days of the test. Therefore, in the summer of 1981, after we moved to the Sierra Nevadas, we took the test again with much better results. We still had some troubles, but they were more subtle and far less devastating.

We kept putting off taking the test again because there was never a convenient time to do it. Finally, we agreed that it would have to be done regardless of convenience. Putting off an essential task because it doesn't easily fit into your plans is a very easy trap to fall into. Don't kid yourself into thinking you are prepared without really taking the test.

One of the first things we encountered in this test was that it's difficult not to cheat. When we had to drive into town twice during the test to keep commitments, we found it really tempting to stop for something cold to drink when it was over ninety-five degrees. Of course, this problem would not have existed in a real emergency situation because there would have been no commitments to take us into town, and no cold drinks available. Our test was colored by the fact that it was very hot during that three-day period and we no longer had access to our air conditioning, ice cubes, and refrigeration.

My attitude on cheating is this. Usually cheating on a test leaves you the loser, but in this case, a little cheating gives you a real appreciation for what you may have to do without someday. On the second sweltering day of the test, we each had one cold glass of root beer, and I have never tasted anything so good. It really made me appreciate civilization and all its amenities.

Now for the good news. Our new portable toilet worked very well and we were quite comfortable with it. The chemicals in the holding tank prevented any smell. We used a two-burner Coleman stove and had plenty of fuel for it. It worked very well, even though we had to do some fancy experimenting when we tried to use the Coleman oven.

We used some paper plates and bowls, and I realized we also needed to store disposable foil pots and pans. We did our test at the time when the many ants in our area emerged, and discovering at ten at night that our kitchen was invaded was not too pleasant. Thereafter, we made sure that all dishes were washed before it got dark. It is much easier then than when you have to heat the water on a camp stove by kerosene light. Using disposable plates and other picnic utensils helps to keep down the number of items that have to be washed. We found we needed at least two medium-sized kettles for heating water for washing, and two pitchers for carrying and pouring water. It isn't convenient to brush your teeth with water from a five-gallon jerry can.

We found that we had made great improvements in lamp selection. We had done a lot of work since our first test, and it showed. In addition to the two kerosene lamps we used the first time, we had two more wick lamps which were easily carried in one hand, and one wick lamp mounted high on the wall in the living room. These made a definite difference in visibility, especially when we lighted them all in one room.

But the real improvement was the addition of the three Aladdin kerosene mantle lamps. They were great—bright and white, and almost as good as electric lights. One Aladdin mantle lamp puts out about ten times as much light as any of our wick lamps. We could easily read by them and didn't feel like we were living in the Dark Ages.

It is a measure of the lamps' success that we did not revert to going to sleep at dark and getting up at dawn. This illumination was sufficient to allow us to set our own time schedules again. That made a big difference. We also had a new mantle lantern with a shade which we used for the first time during the test.

A word of warning is needed here. The mantle lamps, unlike the kerosene wick lamps, do take some special attention after lighting. They tend to get hotter and hotter when first lit and you have to turn them down until they stabilize to prevent carbon build-up on the mantle. We found this out the hard way. Because the mantle of the lamp was concealed by the shade, we did not notice it carbonizing until flames were shooting out of the top of the chimney. We thought the mantle was completely ruined since it was totally black. But we turned the lamp way down, and it slowly burned away the carbon until the mantle was completely clean again. This taught us two lessons: to keep a sharp eye on the lamps, especially those with shades, and not to throw away carbonized mantles.

So our lighting was completely adequate, though we did discover that a room with no windows was almost useless unless we kept a light going in there all day. The Aladdin lamps give off a lot of heat, and keeping one running all day long in June wasn't a good idea. We just about stopped using our bathroom because of its lack of natural illumination. We resorted to using other rooms of the house as the bathroom. We were using a portable toilet, remember.

Bruce's thumb was our main casualty when it came to cooking and lighting. After seventy-two hours of adjusting our new kerosene mantle lanterns and pumping up the Coleman stove, the ball of his right thumb became swollen, blue, and sore. Forewarned is forearmed; make sure you have a pair of pliers and heavy gloves handy to help prevent this problem.

We also gained new understanding of how much water we used. We were not miserly in our use of water, but neither were we extravagant. Even so, we used an average of five gallons of water a day for the three days for two adults and a two-year-old child. I am sure that one of the reasons Bill Pier designed the test to be three days long is that you can't ignore baths for much longer than that. I took a sponge bath which was quite satisfactory and didn't use much water, but I certainly did not feel as relaxed as with a real bath. I did feel clean though. I even washed my hair by being very careful in my use of water. Even so, it took an entire gallon of water for one shampoo. We did not water plants, nor do any cleaning in the house other than dishes, and we still used five gallons per day.

I already mentioned the ants in the kitchen. With a two-year-old trying to feed himself, it was inevitable that the floor got dirty, and although we wiped up the spills, I can tell you that after three days I was glad to be able to wash my kitchen floor. Though you can use a minimum amount of water for a few days, the longer you go, the more water you will need to use. You can't forever put off washing your clothes, diapers, floors, and counters. With the droughts and water problems increasing, it might help you to know that rationing water in many localities consists of limiting each person's water consumption to fifty gallons per day. They call that a limit?

There was one problem we didn't solve in this Three-Day Test: the difficulty of doing without refrigeration.

The moat made by stacking bowls and dishes in a dishpan of water worked well for keeping ants and flies out of our leftovers. We learned, though, that food spoils quickly without refrigeration. Going without refrigeration is like going back centuries. Even Thomas Jefferson owned an icebox.

[THE THREE-DAY TEST]

At first we thought it was kind of romantic, going back to grandmother's era like that. Then we quickly realized that we were not going back only two or three generations, but several *centuries* instead. Even Thomas Jefferson had an icebox, but we had no form of refrigeration at all!

The problem was not just a question of keeping things cool, but also of keeping the bugs, ants, and flies out of them. People used to have root cellars and maybe they worked, but I sure found out quickly that we needed something better than leaving the food out on the counter. I discovered the origins of the parental command, "Clean your plate." Food spoils quickly without refrigeration, especially in the summer, and it only took about an hour for the ants to find the leftovers. We rigged up a washbasin with water in it and stacked bowls of leftovers in the center to frustrate the ants, but I can understand how in olden times leftovers were thrown out or given to the dogs. People then tried to fix only enough food for one meal, but this is a difficult adjustment to make when you are used to storing lots of leftovers.

We didn't have a stream nearby, nor did we have a root cellar, and didn't find a solution to this problem. I can imagine the mess we'd have if our refrigerator was actually turned off. Everything in it would have to be thrown out almost immediately to prevent the ants from taking over the house. If you have an idea what people should do in this situation, short of buying a generator to keep the refrigerator going, please let me know and I will share it with others.

As for some of the psychological problems encountered during our Three-Day Test, taking the test was *not* fun. In fact, I highly recommend a big bottle of aspirin to help soothe frayed nerves. People who are used to air conditioning are not acclimatized to natural summer heat, and don't react well to it. At least we didn't.

I went into the test expecting adventure, but I found everyday, ordinary life—just more difficult than it had been before. I am not particularly good at coping with hardships, which is why I am interested in avoiding as many as possible in the future. We had lights to turn on, but they were harder to light than electric bulbs, and we had to watch them. We had a stove to cook on, but it wasn't as easy to use as our electric stove, and we had to use it outside in case of a fire. We had time to read, but we didn't have the stimulation of TV and radio to keep us occupied. My husband was able to work on his writing, but he had to use a pencil instead of his usual electric typewriter. We had neither refrigeration nor the privilege of going to the store if we needed something. I was very glad when our test was over. I turned on the lights, poured a drink of cold water from the faucet, and flushed the toilet a few times just for fun. I cannot tell you how much more I appreciate the level of civilization we have achieved after doing without it for just three days.

When I was writing this chapter, I asked some acquaintances about their experiences during their tests and they didn't want to talk about them. I don't know whether they ran into trouble like we did, or whether they didn't want to admit that they hadn't tried the Three-Day Test. I hope that you will share your experiences with me as I have shared mine with you. I have learned a great deal from each of my mistakes. Please write to me and let me know what you learned, so we can all make fewer errors in the future. Write to me at Drawer CP-45, Manhattan Beach, CA 90266.

One last note. We are planning to take the test again in the winter because conditions are very different then.

[THE THREE-DAY TEST]

This time we learned to deal with the heat; next time we will try our skills at dealing with the cold.

13. The Bare Necessities

When I first discovered that half the potential emergencies require leaving home for some period of time, I started thinking about what evacuees should take with them in the car. Fortunately, Bruce has several friends who are interested in portable survival kits, and they lent us valuable lists and advice. One thing they pointed out was that even the disasters which would not force you to flee might nevertheless catch you away from home. Even then, though, you would probably be near your car, so having survival materials stored in the trunk is a good idea. One friend refers to his automobile survival kit as "the boogie bag." "You have to be ready to boogie!" he explains.

The list of essential or optional items for the car survival kit quickly burgeoned to an unmanageable size, so I divided it into thirteen separate kits. This makes it easier for you to categorize the items you need and make adjustments to fit your situation. For instance, if you are not going to camp, you will not need the camping kit. I would suggest, however, that even if you are not planning to cook your own meals, you still carry a few days' supply of food with you. You never know what might happen, and you will be much happier if you have some food with you in an emergency.

The thirteen basic kits to assemble for a quick evac-uation by car are: car tools and spare parts, navigation, electronics, clothes, food, medicine, sanitation, per-sonal, money, defense, heavy tools, camping, and last-minute miscellaneous. Remember that you need only put together the kits that fit your needs. Add items that suit you, delete those unsuitable to your situation, and include items you already have in your household sur-vival supplies to avoid duplication. The car medical kit, for instance, can be made up from the household medi-cal kit. The car food supply can be drawn from the household emergency food, and so on. Just don't put off doing it for too long. Your insurance depends on your having everything ready to throw into the car, or already there, in an emergency. You won't have time to put it all together when you need it. You may not be in a very organized state of mind.

Speaking of organization, here's a hint we borrowed from backpacking friends. Go to a backpacking or bicycle-touring store and get a few nylon stuff bags. These waterproof nylon bags with drawstrings come in a variety of colors and sizes and are used by campers to stuff down sleeping bags and parkas into. If you organ-ize your evacuation equipment and supplies by putting different kits in different-colored stuff bags, you can find what you need in a hurry.

Car Kit — Tools and Parts

There are basic tools and spare parts which really ought to be in every car, and especially in every car intended for use as an emergency vehicle. Remember that even if you don't have the skills to use all the tools, someone else who does may stop to help you. This kit is not intended to help you do a tune-up or engine over-haul, but is for hurriedly making repairs at the side of

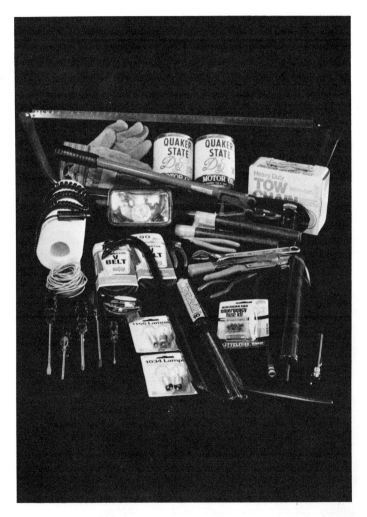

This emergency car kit is designed for minor repairs on the escape route. The bolt cutters, bow saw, and crowbar could make the difference between getting away or being trapped.

the road. With this kit you will be able to fix a flat tire, empty gas tank, low oil level, lack of traction, poor visibility, and a few minor breakdowns. If the problem is major, you'd better hitch a ride with somebody else. The set of tools which must be in your car at all times is that for changing tires. Believe it or not, we have a friend who caused us some inconvenience one time because she had *discarded* her jack and tire iron to make more room in her trunk. First check to be sure that the factory-issue tools are present, then check to see that the spare tire is in good condition and is properly inflated. A flat spare can be very disappointing. If your tire iron is one of those miserable L-shaped rods with a socket welded to the short end of the L, buy a three-foot length of one-inch metal water pipe to use as an extension. You need the pipe to get more leverage for loosening those lug nuts tightened by a mechanic with a pneumatic wrench. Slip the pipe over the end of the tire iron, fit the iron to the nut, and then jump up and down on the end of the pipe to break the nut free. It isn't elegant, but it works.

Once you can change a tire, you should start working on a general repair tool kit. Your car tool kit should contain a set of screwdrivers including Phillips heads and flat-blades in assorted sizes; a pocketknife of the Swiss Army type; two pairs of medium-sized pliers, both regular and needle-nosed; a pair of wire cutters; a set of jumper cables; a small hammer; a vice grip; a crescent wrench; a handheld spotlight powered by the car's cigarette lighter; a towing cable or sturdy rope; a roll of electrical tape; a roll of duct tape; a roll of paper towels; a box of pre-moistened towelettes; a bright orange vest; and a tire pressure gauge and tire pump.

In terms of spare parts, the kit should have a set of windshield wiper blades; two or three quarts of oil; a spare fan-type belt or two; a coil of heavy insulated wire; a set of fuses; several flares; turn and brake light bulbs; a can of cold-start spray if you live in cold country; and a set of tire chains that fits your car if you need to deal with snow or mud.

A two-and-a-half-gallon Explosafe can of the type of gasoline your car uses is a good investment. Imagine yourself rousted out of bed at two in the morning by a flood warning and finding that the car is nearly out of gas. So what if you could have filled it up on the way to work in the morning? Those two and a half gallons will take most modern cars between thirty and eighty miles, which is at least a good start. Carry a dry chemical fire extinguisher too.

Store the tools and spare parts in a small toolbox or stuff bag with the gas can in the trunk of the car. Mount the fire extinguisher within reach of the driver's seat.

Navigation Kit

The navigation kit, though not very big, is extremely important. You have taken precautions so that your car will run, but you need to know where to go. It's important to explore several different routes out of your area, since some of them might be blocked during an emergency. During the floods in Phoenix, Arizona, in 1980, eight out of the ten bridges crossing the river in the middle of the city were closed. Think about this before you and your family are trapped on a closed road.

The best approach is to sit down with a large-scale road map of your area and mark the most direct route from your house to your proposed refuge area. Then drive the route carefully and mark every place where something might block your way, including unplanned obstacles such as fallen bridges. At every potential block, begin an alternate route around the obstacle.

Where the alternate has potential blocks, find additional alternatives. Soon your map will look like a Christmas tree of branching and rebranching routes. This may take you most of a morning or even an entire weekend to do thoroughly, but it's worth it.

This exercise with the map will teach you several things. The first is that there may be bottlenecks in your escape routes. They may all depend on one road down the canyon, or one bridge across the river. You might find a route that was not obvious, but which has no apparent block points. The exercise will teach you something you didn't know about escape routes from your house, and even better, you will find that you will not only have explored the neighborhood, but you will also have memorized the map.

The navigation kit consists of a good compass and maps of the area you are leaving and the areas you will be traveling through to your destination. Street maps are essential, of course, and so are topographic maps that give altitude measurements which could become very important during a flood or heavy snow. Put the compass and maps in a large envelope and store it in the glove compartment of your escape car.

Electronics Kit

The electronics kit consists of radios and flashlights. These items are usually fairly small and relatively fragile, and share the need for batteries. It's usually most convenient to treat them as a single kit.

Once you leave your house in an emergency, you will want to know what is going on. Your car radio will give you news bulletins while you are driving, but you should also have a small battery-powered radio for when you stop and set up your base. A portable weather alert radio is also an excellent idea. Make sure to get one

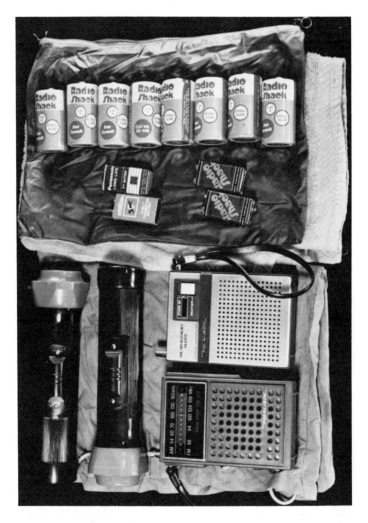

This electronics kit contains an AM-FM radio, a weather alert radio, flashlights, a double set of batteries, and a towel to cushion the radios. Don't store radios and flashlights with batteries inside.

with an alert feature, which will set off a beep in an emergency. It gives continuous weather updating for your area, which is essential in a flood or hurricane.

Once you are stopped, you will have an immediate need for light if it's night. A good-sized flashlight will go a long way in helping you unload what you need from the car and establishing your base. A battery-powered fluorescent lantern is also an excellent tool to have with you. You don't have to carry and point it, and it produces a lot of light. With four 6-volt batteries, it will supply light for several evenings.

The radios and flashlights should be stored in their original boxes, if possible, in a stuff bag, along with a double set of batteries and spare bulbs for the lights. If you don't have good packing for the radios, roll them in a towel to pad them. Keep the kit in the trunk of your car. If you are worried about the batteries going bad, you can put an extra set in the refrigerator, but remember that you might be caught away from home when the disaster strikes. Be sure to put the extra battery set on your last-minute list (see below).

Whatever you do, don't store any equipment with batteries inside. If one battery leaks in the nylon bag, you'll have a mess, but you'll still be able to use the remaining good batteries to power the radios and flashlights. If a battery leaks inside the radio, you've lost the radio. Put the batteries inside a plastic bag in case they leak.

A CB radio installed in the car is most useful, especially if you need to find out what caused the traffic jam ahead, or if you need to call for help. We routinely install CBs in our cars, but strictly speaking it isn't part of the electronics kit.

Clothing Kit

I have listed the clothing kit next in order of importance for one main reason. There may come a time when you will wake up in the middle of the night knee-deep in water or in a blazing house and will need to grab your family and get out as fast as you can. Then is not the time to stop and help everyone put on sensible clothes. So have a clothing kit packed with a complete set of clothing from shoes to underwear for each member of the family. You can pick the kids up in their pajamas and know you have clothes for them. In putting this kit together, keep one thing in mind: It is easier to survive heat with improper clothing than cold. Therefore, a warm set of clothes designed for your particular area is best.

Put each person's clothing kit in a separate stuff bag and label each prominently by name. Pack your clothes so that you can remove them in the order you will need them while dressing, so you won't have to rummage through the bottom of the bag trying to find the underwear. Don't overlook the need to slip a pair of old shoes or boots into the bottom of the bag. By the way, an extra pair of socks is a really good idea too. Put a towel on top of everything so if you just got drenched, you can dry off before dressing. Finally, put an inexpensive rainsuit in the bag, too, or at least stick in a large plastic trash bag. You can cut head and arm holes in a trash bag and use it as a raincoat in a pinch. Store the clothing kits in the trunk of the car.

Food and Water Kit

This kit consists of at least three days' worth of food, the items you need to cook it, and minimal water.

Water presents a problem, since it's so heavy and bulky. Three 5-gallon water cans weigh as much as a

small adult and take up a lot of room in the trunk, not to
mention the effect on your gasoline mileage from day to
day. Most people rightly decide not to carry much water
in their evacuation kit, and rely on two or three 1-quart
canteens or a gallon milk bottle as their water supply.
This is okay, as long as you include a five-gallon folding
plastic water jug in the kit.

Once you are out of the danger area, you can stop
almost anywhere and ask someone to let you fill up your
water jug. You don't have to carry several gallons of
water in the car all the time, but you must have the
ability to do so in a pinch. A folding water jug is very
handy for that. Make sure you have some halazone
tablets with you in case the water you find is of questionable purity which is about all the water you can find
these days. During floods even municipal water sys-
tems become contaminated with sewage.

When deciding on what food to pack, the considera-
tions are much like those made in storing food at home.
In fact, taking half of the recommended one-week
canned food supply mentioned in chapter 2 will just
about do it. Freeze-dried food will be much lighter, but
canned foods will give you more liquid and do not need
to be heated. They are cheaper too. Buy food in containers of the size that your family will consume all in one
meal. You should probably bring along some canned
fruit juices to supplement the water supply, too.

We bring along our MSR stove (mentioned in chapter
5) for cooking our food in an emergency. It is small and
lightweight, taking up very little room. We take a quart
of kerosene with us, because it's the least explosive fuel,
but it will use a variety of fuels. Don't forget those
necessities such as matches, can openers, hot pads,
paper plates, cups, pots, silverware, and napkins. A
sponge and dishwashing soap will make the cleanup

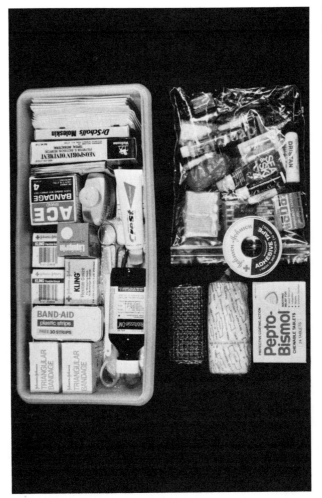

Our evacuation medical kit is a Tupperware breadbox which contains all the medical materials we are likely to need in three days.

much easier, though I use as many disposable items as possible. Three days' worth of disposables doesn't take up much room.

Depending on what you put in your food and water kit, you may be able to store it in a stuff bag or you may have to resort to a cardboard box to hold the heavy canned goods. In either case, be sure to store the kit in the trunk of the car.

Medical Kit

In chapter 6, I recommend several emergency-care books and their medical kits. I also recommend the excellent and extensive Rescue Pac paramedic bandage kit. However, you might find this to be too much for your car medical kit. We have put together a car medical kit that fits into a Tupperware bread container. Add to this list any daily medications members of your family have to take. Our kit contains a zippered plastic bag for small items which include decongestant inhaler, lip balm, caffeine tablets, tincture of Merthiolate vials, suntan lotion or sunscreen, liquid soap, Sting Kill swabs, halazone tablets, toothache drops, snakebite kit, salt tablets, waterproof matches, needle and thread, and safety pins. This bag rests on top of the larger objects in the kit which are cough syrup, toilet paper, scissors, surgical clamp, four sanitary napkins, two triangular bandages, one box assorted Band-Aids, six butterfly closures, one wire splint, two 2-inch gauze rolls, two 3-inch gauze rolls, one 4-inch ace bandage, tablets for upset stomach, pain-reliever tablets, one-inch adhesive tape, six 3-inch square sterile pads, antibacterial ointment, aspirin for children, disinfectant soap, moleskin, six pre-moistened towelettes, six 3-by-5-inch sterile pads, and six large eye pads.

Just before writing this chapter we put this kit together and took a two-week car trip. I was quite surprised when I discovered that we used several of the items right away. At the beginning of our trip, the water system in our camper developed a leak and we used our adhesive tape to fix it temporarily. Then at the end of the trip, we developed some intestinal trouble and were very grateful for the baby aspirin and the upset stomach tablets. Then when we ran out of baby wipes, we were quite pleased to discover we had the pre-moistened towelettes in the kit. It helped a lot and this wasn't even a disaster, just a vacation.

If possible, store the medical kit inside the car where you can reach it, otherwise keep it in the trunk. Be sure to check the tablets in the kit during cold weather. Condensation inside the bottles may disintegrate the tablets.

Sanitation Kit

As I said earlier in the book, portable toilets are handy items but they are very bulky and may not be easy to store in the trunk of a car. You might consider going to a sporting goods store and buying a very inexpensive potty stool, which is a folding camp stool with a familiar looking seat and a plastic bag hanging underneath. When you are done, you just remove the plastic bag and dispose of it. You can also dig a hole and set the stool over it, which eliminates unfamiliar squatting. We have found this type of sanitary arrangement to be unsatisfactory in general, but far better than nothing. Store the potty stool and a dozen bags in the trunk of the car. A backpacker's small plastic trowel will be useful if you have no other digging tools. And don't forget TP.

[URBAN ALERT!]

Personal Kit

This kit is filled with those things we take for granted, but would be lost without. It is basically a personal hygiene kit, containing toothbrushes, toothpaste, comb and hairbrush, razor, soap, shampoo, sanitary napkins, spare set of glasses, cotton swabs, washcloths and towels, makeup, shampoo, deodorant, needle and thread, pencil and paper, and a small mirror.

The way to discover whether you left items out of this kit is to take everything you use when you wash up in the morning, and set it aside. If something that you use all the time is not on the list put it on. Having an extra of each of these items tucked away in this kit really comes in handy if you run out. More than once we have supplied a houseguest with a new toothbrush or razor without having to drive into town. Just remember to replace anything you take from the kit.

Spread these items on a bath towel and then carefully roll it up and put it in a stuff bag. Rolling the items in the towel will pad them and keep them from rattling against one another. Store the bag in the trunk of the car.

Money Kit

These days going anywhere without money is difficult, to say the least. But especially in an emergency, when you are not in a bargaining position, you had better have some cash available. I suggest you keep some money in a money kit.

This kit should consist of three different kinds of money. Firstly, you should have at least a hundred dollars in bills no larger than five-dollar bills. If you need something inexpensive and the other guy doesn't have change, you don't want to have to spend twenty

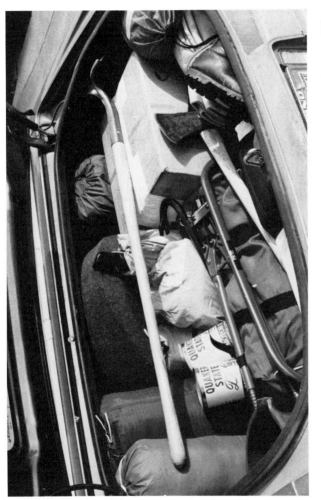

The 13 survival kits for emergency evacuation easily fit in the trunk of a car. Kits shown here are sufficient to sustain a family of three for three days. The kits allow a family to flee at a moment's notice.

dollars for it. You can always pay for expensive things with several fives. Secondly, you should have a roll of dimes and another of quarters so you can make phone calls to friends or relatives. It might be a little hard to go hunting for change in a hurricane. Thirdly, in today's society a good backup is to have a VISA or MasterCard along with two or three gasoline credit cards in the kit. Sometimes people will accept them more readily than cash. My husband went shopping the other day and paid for something with several twenty-dollar bills. Before accepting his cash, they wanted to see his driver's license and a major credit card! It's a sign of the times.

When determining how much money to have stashed away, don't forget the rising price of gas. If you are planning to drive very far, consider the availability of the gas and what it is going to cost you in a crisis.

Get an old wallet and stuff it with the cash and credit cards, then put it in a small stuff bag or heavy envelope with the rolls of coins. Keep it in the glove compartment of the car with the navigation kit.

Defense Kit

These kits are intended mainly for emergency evacuations or self-sufficiency when the emergency catches you away from home. The emergencies we have discussed have mainly been impersonal, not the kind for which you would need a gun. On the other hand, sometimes it's comforting to have a gun, and if you were caught away from home in a riot zone, it could be very, very comforting. What should be in your defense kit?

For a car defense kit, probably the best policy is to have a .45 pistol, a holster and belt, three magazines, and a box of fifty cartridges, all kept in a waterproof bag or other small container. Although there are a few parts of the country where it is illegal to own a pistol, in most areas a gun locked in the trunk of a car is permitted. If not, it's extremely unlikely that the average person's trunk will be searched by a law officer anyway. So stick the defense kit in your trunk and stop running red lights. Get it out only when the danger posed by not having it at hand is greater than the danger posed by being caught with it by the authorities.

Heavy Tool Kit

What if you need to break a padlocked chain to get to high ground in a flood? What if there is a tree lying across the road and you have to move it? What if you need to pry through wreckage or dig through mud when you return to your home? What if you want to help fight the wildfire that is threatening your house? How will you dig a latrine or bury your garbage if you have to camp out? Obviously there should be some room for heavy-duty tools in your evacuation kit too.

I suggest that you start with the basic three: ax, bucket, and shovel. These are basic firefighting tools which happen to be good for flood-fighting, too, if you use full-sized tools, not miniatures. Don't succumb to the temptation to throw an old Army trenching tool in the trunk and call it a shovel; nor is a hatchet an ax. Throw in a pair of heavy bolt cutters if there is any possibility that a locked gate will bar your way out of the danger area. A hand saw, preferably one of the folding backpack or pruning saws, will help you deal with fallen trees and branches. A heavy crowbar is good insurance too. Just tuck them away in the bottom of the trunk. It won't hurt them to rattle around a little.

Camping Kit

If your evacuation plans include the possibility of having to camp out, you will need at least a tent, and

possibly other items of equipment. Since we go backpacking now and then, we just use our lightweight two-
man tent in its stuff sack. Although you could shelter
your family by having them sleep in the car, that gets
old fast. A tent lets you stretch out flat and really rest,
something a compact car bucket seat usually won't do.

For sleeping on the ground inside the tent, you'll need
sleeping bags, blankets, pillows, and above all, compressed foam insulation or padding to put *under* your
body. This isn't for softness, although it provides that,
but to keep your body heat from draining into the cold
ground. We use Ensolite pads from the backpacking
store, which are a kind of hard foam rubber about half
an inch thick. They provide excellent insulation and
will not absorb water from the ground. There are other
kinds of sleeping pads available, but don't make the
mistake of using air mattresses, since these are almost
always troublesome and do not provide much insulation. But be sure to use something between you and the
ground, or you'll be miserably cold and sleepless.

My suggestion is to store your family members'
sleeping bags and tent in the trunk of your car where
they will be available, or at the very least make a note
on your last-minute list (see below) to take your pillows,
sheets, blankets, and towels with you in the car. Rip
them right off the beds on your way out the door. Take
the shower curtains too. That way you can be warm
and dry even if you don't have sleeping bags.

Last-Minute Kit

The last-minute kit is the one I mentioned in chapter
10. Even in a five-minute evacuation, there will be
certain items around the house that you will really want
to take with you, like the photo album, legal documents,
your parakeet, jewelry, or whatever has special value

to you but which wouldn't be reasonably kept in the trunk of the car in an emergency kit.

Take a large canvas or nylon duffle bag and store it in the hall closet near the front door. A bag which opens at one end and has a shoulder strap is best. Use a large safety pin to pin an extra set of car keys to the bag, and attach a list of everything you want to take with you at the last minute, organized on a room-by-room basis. Then when the crisis occurs, you can grab the bag, pin the keys to the front of your shirt where you can see them, and move quickly from one room to another tossing things into the bag as you go down the list. That way when you join the rest of the family at the car, you will have both your valuables and your car keys.

When selecting the items for your last-minute list, try to take only the things that will be irreplaceable. Big, bulky items like TV sets can usually be replaced by insurance. It takes only money. But money can't replace your family pictures, financial records, legal documents, and keepsakes.

Appendix A— Check List for Home

This checklist includes items which are essential for meeting an extended disaster at home. The list is a summary of the information in chapters 2 through 8.

Food

☐ _____ weeks' food for _____ people = _____ person-weeks (canned, freeze-dried, air-dried or basic four)

Water

☐ 2 gallons/person/day x _____ days x _____ persons = _____ gallons, and water purifier

Sanitary Supplies

☐ portable toilet
☐ deodorizing chemicals
☐ special toilet paper
☐ shampoo
☐ toothpaste
☐ toothbrushes (including extras)
☐ mouthwash
☐ soap
☐ deodorant
☐ dishwashing detergent
☐ toilet paper
☐ facial tissues

- ☐ paper towels
- ☐ paper napkins
- ☐ razor blades
- ☐ laundry soap
- ☐ cotton swabs
- ☐ sanitary napkins
- ☐ disposable diapers
- ☐ plastic garbage bags

Light and Heat

- ☐ flashlight
- ☐ extra batteries
- ☐ mantle lanterns
- ☐ fuel for mantle lanterns: _____ hours/night x _____ nights x _____ ounces/hour consumption = _____ ounces kerosene
- ☐ Explosafe cans
- ☐ stove
- ☐ fuel for stove: _____ cooking hours/day x _____ days x _____ ounces/hour consumption = _____ ounces kerosene
- ☐ fire extinguishers

Cooking Supplies

- ☐ plates
- ☐ bowls
- ☐ cups
- ☐ pots and pans
- ☐ 2 pitchers
- ☐ 2 saucepans

Medical Supplies

- ☐ *A Sigh of Relief*
- ☐ *How To Be Your Own Doctor (Sometimes)*
- ☐ *Family Health and Home Nursing*

[APPENDIX A — CHECKLIST FOR HOME]

- ☐ *Where There Is No Doctor*
- ☐ *The Ship's Medicine Chest and Medical Aid At Sea*
- ☐ medical supplies
- ☐ daily prescriptions
- ☐ dental kit
- ☐ Rescue Pac or other first aid kit

Entertainment

- ☐ books
- ☐ games
- ☐ crafts

Radios

- ☐ AM-FM-Shortwave
- ☐ weather radio
- ☐ public service scanner
- ☐ CB - Channel 9 crystals

Defense

- ☐ shotgun
- ☐ ammunition for shotgun

Do Your Three-Day Test

Appendix B—
Check List for Car Evacuation

This checklist is a summary of the evacuation kits described in chapter 13.

Car Kit — Tools and Parts

☐ jack and tire iron
☐ good spare tire
☐ three-foot section of one-inch metal water pipe
☐ screwdrivers—Phillips head and flat-blade in assorted sizes
☐ pocketknife (Swiss Army type)
☐ pliers—regular and needle-nosed
☐ wire cutters
☐ jumper cables
☐ small hammer
☐ vice grip
☐ crescent wrench
☐ spotlight (handheld powered by car's cigarette lighter)
☐ towing cable or sturdy rope
☐ electrical tape
☐ duct tape
☐ paper towels
☐ pre-moistened towelettes
☐ orange vest
☐ tire pressure gauge

- ☐ tire pump
- ☐ windshield wiper blades
- ☐ 2 quarts of oil
- ☐ fan-type belts
- ☐ heavy insulated wire
- ☐ fuses
- ☐ flares
- ☐ light bulbs (turn and brakes)
- ☐ cold-start spray
- ☐ tire chains
- ☐ 2½-gallon Explosafe can of gasoline

Navigation Kit

- ☐ large-scale road map of your area
- ☐ maps of areas you will be traveling through
- ☐ compass
- ☐ topographic maps

Electronics Kit

- ☐ portable weather alert radio
- ☐ portable AM-FM radio
- ☐ flashlights
- ☐ battery-powered fluorescent lantern
- ☐ extra batteries
- ☐ spare light bulbs for lights
- ☐ CB radio

Clothing Kit

For each person
- ☐ towel
- ☐ underwear
- ☐ socks
- ☐ pants
- ☐ shirt
- ☐ shoes

[APPENDIX B — CHECKLIST FOR CAR EVACUATION]

☐ jacket
☐ rain gear

Food and Water Kit

☐ 2 one-quart canteens or one-gallon milk bottles
☐ folding five-gallon plastic water jug
☐ halazone tablets
☐ food: _____ persons x 3 days = _____
person-days supply
☐ stove
☐ fuel for stove
☐ matches
☐ can opener
☐ hot pad
☐ paper plates
☐ cups
☐ pots
☐ silverware
☐ napkins
☐ sponge
☐ dishwashing soap

Medical Kit

Small items:
☐ decongestant inhaler
☐ lip balm
☐ caffeine tablets
☐ tincture of Merthiolate
☐ suntan lotion or sunscreen
☐ liquid soap
☐ Sting Kill swabs
☐ halazone tablets
☐ toothache drops
☐ snakebite kit
☐ salt tablets

☐ waterproof matches
☐ needle and thread
☐ safety pins
Larger items:
☐ cough syrup
☐ toilet paper (small roll)
☐ scissors
☐ surgical clamp
☐ 4 sanitary napkins (as bandages)
☐ 2 triangular bandages
☐ box assorted Band-Aids
☐ 6 butterfly closures
☐ wire splint
☐ 2 two-inch gauze rolls
☐ 2 three-inch gauze rolls
☐ 1 four-inch ace bandage
☐ tablets for upset stomach
☐ pain reliever tablets
☐ 1-inch adhesive tape roll
☐ 6 three-inch-square sterile pads
☐ antibacterial ointment
☐ aspirin for children
☐ disinfectant soap
☐ moleskin
☐ 6 pre-moistened towelettes
☐ 6 three-by-four-inch sterile pads
☐ 6 eye pads
☐ daily medications

Sanitation Kit

☐ potty stool and bags
☐ small shovel or trowel
☐ toilet paper

[APPENDIX B — CHECKLIST FOR CAR EVACUATION]

Personal Kit

- ☐ toothbrushes
- ☐ toothpaste
- ☐ comb and hairbrush
- ☐ razor
- ☐ soap
- ☐ shampoo
- ☐ sanitary napkins
- ☐ spare set of glasses
- ☐ mirror
- ☐ cotton swabs
- ☐ washcloths and towels
- ☐ makeup
- ☐ shampoo
- ☐ deodorant
- ☐ needle and thread
- ☐ pencil and paper
- ☐ bath towel

Money Kit

- ☐ $100 in five-dollar bills
- ☐ roll of dimes
- ☐ roll of quarters
- ☐ VISA or MasterCard
- ☐ gas credit cards

Defense Kit

- ☐ .45 pistol
- ☐ holster and belt
- ☐ 3 magazines
- ☐ 50 cartridges

Heavy Tool Kit

- ☐ ax
- ☐ bucket

[URBAN ALERT!]

- ☐ shovel
- ☐ heavy bolt cutters
- ☐ hand saw
- ☐ crowbar

Camping Kit

- ☐ tent
- ☐ sleeping bags (one per person)
- ☐ blankets
- ☐ pillows
- ☐ compressed foam pad

Last-Minute Kit

- ☐ duffle bag
- ☐ list
- ☐ car keys
- ☐ photos
- ☐ legal documents
- ☐ pets
- ☐ jewelry